PORTABLE COMPUTING

Grateful acknowledgment is made to the following for permission to reproduce illustrations:

GRiD Systems Corporation, Figures 1-1 and 6-6
Quicksoft, Figure 4-1
Alan Freedman, author of *The Computer Glossary,* Figures 6-1 and 10-1
James R. Stroh of LXD, Inc., also for Figure 6-1
Reflection Technology, Figures 6-2 and 6-3
Kirk MacKenzie and ProHance Technologies, Inc., Figure 6-5
Weltec Digital, Inc., Figure 7-1
Compaq Computer Corporation, Figures 7-2 and 10-2
Eastman Kodak Company, Figure 8-1
Ricoh Corporation, Figure 8-2
Zenith Data Systems, Figures 9-1, 9-4, and 9-5
Gates Energy Products, Figure 9-2
Traveling Software, Figures 6-4 and 9-3
Anthro Corporation, Figure 10-3
Curtis Manufacturing Company, Figure 10-4
Pace Cases, Figures 10-6, 10-8, and 10-9
Product R&D Corporation, Figure 10-7

PORTABLE COMPUTING
Work on the Go

COLIN HAYNES

amacom

American Management Association

This publication is designed to provide accurate and authoritative
information in regard to the subject matter covered. It is sold with
the understanding that the publisher is not engaged in rendering
legal, accounting, or other professional service. If legal advice or
other expert assistance is required, the services of a competent
professional person should be sought.

Library of Congress Cataloging-in-Publication Data
Haynes, Colin.
    Portable computing : work on the go / Colin Haynes.
       p.   cm.
    Includes bibliographical references and index.
    ISBN 0-8144-7747-X (pbk.)
    1. Office practice—Automation. 2. Portable computers. 3. Quality of work life.
4. Time management. 5. White collar workers—Effect of technological innovations on.
I. Title.
    HF5548.H38   1991
    651.8—dc20   90-53317
                                                                                 CIP

Portable Computing: Work on the Go *is in no way affiliated or endorsed by* Portable
Computing *magazine published by IDG / Peterborough of Peterborough, New Hampshire.*

Printing number

10 9 8 7 6 5 4 3 2 1

There is more to life than increasing its speed.
—Mahatma Gandhi

To
Rebecca, Robert, and James,
as they explore the fascinations of computing.

Contents

Introduction

Welcome to the world of portable computing, probably the most significant technology of our rapidly changing Information Age. Scarcely a decade ago, affordable personal desktop computers (PCs) gave us the power to process knowledge and data electronically, extending our capacity to do more work smarter and to automate many routine tasks. Now that PCs have acquired another dimension—mobility—we begin to see far-ranging changes in both how and where people work. The personal computer can do many things. The portable computer can do even more—because it can function virtually anywhere.

This book combines the how and why of portable computing to enable you to move forward with your own ideas in putting this remarkable new technology to work. The aim is to ensure that you can either get the best value in the most appropriate system for your needs when you buy a portable, or, if you already have the equipment, you can adapt it to form a system that serves you better. In either case, the information in this book should save you a great deal of money and hassle.

In the process of building a portable computer system, we need to think creatively and not just logically about how to apply the technology. That is why this book is much more than just a buyer's guide for portable hardware and software. It is also an idea generator and a database. My intent is to stimulate a reappraisal of traditional ways of working and to show new approaches to managing the computer as a valuable resource for both your business and your personal life.

If your perceptions of the usefulness of portable computers are restrained by conventional applications, then you risk missing many opportunities to do things differently and better. Portable computers can revolutionize the way we interact with machines in general and with computers in particular. Only if you are open to new ways of using these computers can you fully exploit their potential applications, especially when the physical limitations imposed by the present keyboard and screen are eliminated. I discuss many such innovations throughout the book, as a way of showing just how rapidly this area of computing is developing to meet people's needs.

Computing technology has given us the power to work and manage more efficiently, but we are still not fully exploiting the opportunity. The U.S. Department of Labor productivity index for the American work force fell again at the beginning of 1990. But making computers portable can lead to personal computing's delayed productivity payoff by giving the technology more flexible dimensions in place and time.

The addition of mobility can change life-styles, both at work and at home. The divisions between work time and place and private time and place are becoming blurred. This may give us back some of the social and familial strengths that we enjoyed when we were predominantly an agrarian society. Senior citizens, mothers working at home, and the handicapped may benefit especially from this new phase of the information revolution.

The portable office offers us freedom to work when and where we please, to realize our aspirations to set up and run our own businesses, to pursue business and leisure interests, and to create more time.

■ Chapter 1 explores the concept of the portable office and the forms it will take. Chapter 10 concludes with practical advice on putting the elements of a portable office together. The chapters in between detail how to assemble a portable computer system—the software, hardware, and peripherals.

■ Chapter 2 helps you assess your computer needs, with a series of checklists to help define the system most appropriate to your requirements.

■ Chapters 3 and 4 identify your software needs, with particular attention to the integrated software packages so practical for many portable applications.

■ Chapter 5 reviews the many varieties of computers available, from vest-pocket appointment books to full-scale portables more powerful than most desktops.

■ Chapter 6 examines what can be the most frustrating elements of a laptop—the screen and keyboard. Exciting developments are taking place to improve the interfaces between humans and machines, further expanding the applications for portable computing.

■ Chapter 7 samples the computer horsepower situation—the memory and storage capacity and the operating speeds that are mistakenly the focus of so much misleading marketing hype.

■ Chapter 8 discusses peripherals. We take a realistic look at accessories that are cost-effective.

■ Chapter 9 investigates batteries and alternative sources of energy to power portables.

■ Chapter 10 brings it all together—in a carry-on bag or docked on a wheeled unit that you push between work locations. There are mobile units that allow you to transform a kitchen into an office in a few minutes after the children leave for school, then convert it back to family use as quickly at the end of the day.

■ The Appendixes are for readers with special interests. They offer information on computer viruses, health hazards of computer work, electronic mail, how handicapped people can use computers, and the pros and cons of dedicated word processors. The concluding resources section contains a list of manufacturers and suppliers of portable computer equipment and services.

In addition to being a comprehensive briefing on all aspects of the technology, this book covers also the much neglected human resources perspective of computing. There are tips to help you better manage others, as well as make your own work-to-go more productive and enjoyable.

1

The Portable Office

Portable computers offer us a great adventure: a new way of working and living. But we will lose this opportunity to enhance our work and personal lives if we regard them as mere extensions or accessories of desktop systems. They are far more than that. Laptops offer the opportunity to take a fresh look at *how, where,* and *when* we work. The door is opening to many new ways of working, and creating opportunities for fundamental changes in habits that have persisted since the industrial revolution.

There are almost as many portable computer applications as there are users. You may simply add mobility to office-bound data processing tasks, or you may take your computing power out of your office, factory, or warehouse and on to the road (Figure 1-1). For example, Ciba-Geigy medical sales representatives use portable computers in their cars to call up a profile of the physicians they are about to visit.

"The ability to take a computer with you has already had a significant effect on the way that the world does business and the freedom to be obtained from personal computing is a chain reaction that is only just beginning," says Craig Patchett, executive editor of *PC Laptop.* "Over the next decade, the wall that restrains the majority of the people of this planet from the power and freedom that computers offer will continue to crumble as machines get smaller, lighter, less expensive, and, most important, easier to use."

That is why many experts forecast that sales of portables will overtake those of desktops in the 1990s and will become the major growth area of computing.

1

Figure 1-1.   Computing power out of the office.

New Uses for Computers

Among the preconceptions we need to overcome is that a portable computer is a laptop limited to such stereotypical applications as running spreadsheets on an aircraft. Laptops are not just for journalists to prepare copy away from the office, or for sales reps to process orders while on the road. These activities are important, but they represent a very small proportion of the potential use of laptops and other types of portable computers.

Even the name *laptop* is a misnomer, since it is almost impossible to use these computers on your lap (although in Chapter 10 you will find some tips to make this easier). Nor will most laptops function well on the tables fitted to aircraft seats, or have the battery power to last a long flight. That is why so few laptops are actually used on aircraft; the manufacturers still promote that image, but flight attendants know better. Surveys indicate that most laptops are operated over 90 percent of the time within reach of an electrical outlet, so concern about batteries may be a misconception, too.

The term "portable office" is not limited to systems for clerical work, but extends to all activities that can benefit from a combination of computerization and mobility. Composers, engineers, writers, researchers, and consultants of various kinds, investors, medical specialists—all these and many more seek portable equipment that can be set up away from conventional offices and other formal working environments. They want systems at reasonable cost and that are, above all else, easy to use.

- A plumber can transform his business if he has a portable office in his truck so that he can print out estimates and invoices on the spot. He solves most of his cash-flow problems because, by presenting a formal invoice the moment he finishes the job, he can usually collect payment before he leaves the site.
- A legal team in the middle of a complex product liability trial can use a portable office that is enormously powerful in its ability to look up references in a CD-ROM–based library, but has little need for equipment that is very sophisticated or expensive.
- A portable office can be taken to the middle of the biggest cornfield in the Midwest, where a combine harvester has broken down, with 200 acres still to go and storm clouds brewing. The portable office is in a technician's truck, and includes all the service manuals and parts lists on CD-ROM discs. The technician can get immediate help to

diagnose the fault and can order spare parts over a radio data communications link.

There is an enormous variety of such portable office situations. While personal desktop computers have changed the *way* we work, portable computers can drastically change *how, where,* and *when* we perform tasks or solve problems.

Innovative New Design Features

Many must work away from car or desk, in situations where there is no practical place to rest a traditional computer, as when power company technicians capture data from customers' electric meters. Portables must record and process data in situations where operating a keyboard is impossible. Those can range from monitoring merchandise displays and pricing in a supermarket to accessing complex technical specifications at the top of a building still under construction.

Such challenging work environments focus attention on the two most criticized features of portable computers that reflect the compromises necessary in their screen displays and keyboards. The displays tend to be difficult to read and the keyboards are frustrating to operate, because manufacturers often make unsatisfactory trade-offs between weight, battery consumption, size, legibility, and ease of use. But creative engineering is solving these problems. You may no longer need to peer at tiny characters on a screen or peck away at a keyboard, although for many tasks cramped keyboards and conventional displays will continue to be appropriate.

Chapter 6 shows that the keyboard—that antique human-machine interface device—is becoming redundant in some situations. Writing on—or simply touching—the computer screen is now a practical technique. The touch-screen interface is at the heart of new ways of handling information that require little training. It can eliminate the mouse and keyboard, or call the keyboard to the screen when you wish to communicate in the conventional way.

You can also interface with a computer by talking to it—and receive the machine's responses—with steadily improving voice recognition and simulation devices. Most spreadsheets, word processors, and other applications will accept spoken input.

Such innovations open up fascinating new perspectives on the mobility and practicality of computing in difficult situations. We can even compare data and make decisions using a display that integrates visually with real-life situations. You wear a device over one eye that contains a transparent image of the computer display. Such devices are discussed in Chapter 6.

For example, an anesthetist can keep her attention focused on the unconscious patient in the operating room while monitoring readouts of vital signs that appear projected before her eyes. An aircraft technician wedged into position in the landing-gear bay of a jumbo jet can access the drawings he needs from among the literally tons of technical documentation created for such a complex machine. An attorney at a trial who suddenly needs a document or an obscure legal reference can have it faxed before his eyes—from the other side of the country or the world. By linking portable computers to new developments in communications technology, we can now receive and transmit information to and from almost anywhere. Again, a discussion of such new devices appears in Chapter 6, along with illustrations.

The Human Factor: People

Too often, computing is regarded as having only two basic elements: the hardware that is the machinery and the software, or programming, that makes the machinery perform tasks. More important than either is the third, organic, element: people. Many managers still view computers as tools to help people complete routine tasks more efficiently. In fact, portable computers present opportunities for new ways of structuring our working lives, creating bonus time and enhancing the quality of both work and leisure.

The human impact of personal computing has been immense, but you haven't seen anything until you explore the greater possibilities that come when computing acquires mobility. Fundamental changes will occur in the way organizations function, based on the power that portable computing gives us to process data so flexibly and quickly, virtually anywhere, at any time.

Unlike money, time is a finite resource. You cannot print more of it; you cannot run a time deficit the way you can borrow against future income. Time is our most precious commodity—and it is the commodity of the future. It is a driving force behind the portable office trend, because portable computers can shorten the time spent earning money and can create more time for quality living.

Management's Human Resources Solutions

People are the most important asset in any organization, and the most challenging management problem of the 1990s will be finding and keeping the right people. Portable computing offers tangible help in maximizing a company's return on its investment in human resources by expanding those resources as well as by making them more productive.

The Home Office

Employers can attract better caliber staff far more easily if they are not so limited in matching the often conflicting need to live in one place and work in another. Companies now can offer a viable alternative to commuting. For example, state agencies in California are conducting pioneering trials to demonstrate that most jobs—not just a select few—can be done away from the traditional centralized workplace. The means for accomplishing this? Portable computers and telecommunication equipment combined for telecommuting.

Telecommuting must increase. We have no choice. Traffic congestion is expected to at least double, and perhaps triple, by the year 2000. According to the Road Information Program of Washington, D.C., traffic congestion will add an hour to each working day for the typical California commuter, as well as an average individual cost of $5,238 a year in wasted time and gasoline. Nationwide, there are similar problems compounded by the decentralization of urban centers, creating suburban as well as city-center gridlock.

But reducing commuting is not the only motivation for the explosive growth in home offices. I live in the Sausalito houseboat community near San Francisco, an area that is a trendsetter in home offices and where a premium is placed on leisure and life-style. All around me are people in home offices who are writing books, designing furniture, practicing law, programming computers, creating graphic designs, doing major financial deals, and pursuing a host of other occupations. One of my neighbors is Ted Nelson, Autodesk's senior fellow, who is turning his Project Xanadu hypertext concept into reality with the aid of a miscellany of mobile computing tools.

The main benefit reported by those who set up home offices is a reduction in stress—not just in commuting stress but in all work-related problems. The prevailing medical advice is that the best preventive medicine for stress is to enjoy what you are doing. The portable computer makes it easier to achieve that happy condition.

There are surprising aspects of home work that demonstrate what a strong evolutionary trend this is. Studies reveal that employees who operate successfully from home tend to be more loyal to their organizations. But I suspect this statistic is influenced by the fact that organizations with the enterprise and flexibility to create such opportunities are also better at holding on to their people in other respects as well.

Having employees work at home can save a company costs in employee benefits and office overhead. Greater productivity can be achieved in more attractive working environments that blend work with quality leisure time. Productivity can leap—even double—in some cases. The human resources experts emphasize, however, that home-office employees must be strong on self-management, well motivated, and able to function in isolation, without a continuing need for interaction with co-workers.

The home office movement is forcing managers to reevaluate some fundamental management practices. The technology that makes the home office feasible must be integrated with the human resources management skills necessary to make new ways of working effective. Just as we learned from the auto assembly lines, the self-motivated, self-managed worker is the most productive. As the trend toward home offices and telecommuting increases, companies also must adapt to becoming fragmented organizations heavily dependent on out-workers. Their remote computer users still have to be integrated into a centralized organizational structure.

A New Labor Pool

The generations entering the business environment are becoming as wedded to their portable computers as previous generations were to fountain pens and pocket calculators. Young people are not only becoming computer literate at a faster rate, but they are also highly experienced in computing on the trot. Universities regard portables as such useful learning tools that some include the cost of one in their tuition fees, or at least recommend certain models and make them available at deep discounts in college bookstores. The trend toward portable computing in education is extending down from the colleges to the high schools. Consequently, there will be upward pressure from the education system into the business world, as graduates expect to continue to have access to an essential personal information management tool.

At the other end of the age spectrum, it is particularly exciting how, as companies tackle their need for quality workers in the 1990s, they begin to make better use of older people. This expanding sector of our graying population has by no means been left out of the information revolution. Its members are now proving far more enthusiastic about the technology than was the case only a few years ago.

A significant proportion of portable computer buyers are senior citizens. They are learning new skills that they can blend with their priceless experience to make useful contributions without sacrificing the personal freedom they have come to value in retirement.

Another group that will benefit tremendously from this new management perspective is young mothers, traditionally at home during their intellectually as well as physically most productive years. Now that the power of computing can be brought so easily to them in their homes, they can pursue careers more readily, without compromising their child-rearing and home-building roles.

It is particularly significant that proportionately more women than men surveyed say that they intend to buy portable computers. At present, men make over 80 percent of computer buying decisions and have dominated most aspects of personal computing. The portable, with its distinctive character and applications, could greatly influence the emancipation of computing, giving women a more equal role in the design, manufacture, and application of this technology.

Perhaps the greatest freedom and power will be gained by the handicapped, for whom compact and mobile computers can compensate for physical disabilities, opening up greater employment possibilities. A portable computer with voice reproduction programming and hardware has given us access to the brilliant mind of Stephen M. Hawking, the Oxford don and author of the best-selling *A Brief History of Time: From the Big Bang to Black Holes* (New York: Bantam, 1988). His has been a dramatic demonstration of the benefits of portable computing technology.

Portable computing can empower millions of handicapped people to extend and enhance the quality of their lives. This is a major challenge, as well as benefit, for the business community, which has moral and social responsibilities—and growing legislative pressure—to bring more handicapped people into productive roles. The portable computer can provide a highly cost-effective aid to meeting federal requirements, and can turn many handicapped people into extremely valuable employees. (There is more about computing equipment and software for handicapped persons in Appendix D.)

Misspent Monies/Outdated Management

Nearly $9 billion will probably be spent on portable computing in 1991. It is the fastest growing, most important aspect of computing, yet one still plagued by confusion and a lack of readily available quality information on which to base buying decisions. There are many misconceptions about how this exciting new technology should be deployed. As a result, much of that $9 billion will be badly spent on wrong equipment.

Never before has the business community been offered such a far-reaching technology without, at the same time, sufficient enlightenment about how to select and use it. The computing professionals tend not to have the necessary expertise in human resources matters, while the human resources specialists battle to understand the technology. Portable computers are not an automatic passport to greater efficiency, as was demonstrated when the Internal Revenue Service bought over 15,000 machines for their field auditors.

"The General Accounting Office found the thousands of laptops added nothing more to the IRS' bottom line than 15,000 cow pies would have done," comments *Portable Computing*'s West Coast editor Jeff Angus.

The bad IRS experience of laptops was not due to the technology, but caused primarily by a number of human factors in the way the project was managed and the negative attitudes among many of the auditors who had to use the computers. Throughout every type of business—and among people who buy computers for personal use—the potential benefits of the technology too often fail to be realized. Usually the hardware or software choices are not appropriate to either the tasks to be done or to the needs and skills of the people who will actually use the computers.

"The true advantages of portable computer use through an organization may be indirect, intangible, or involved in a complex of variables."

Lack of specialist knowledge about both computers and human behavior, and how they react when brought together, lie at the root of most corporate computing problems. Comments consultant Robert M. Thacker in *Computerworld*: "As we have attempted to renovate companies through the unplanned, uncoordinated, incremental implementation of computer and automation technology, we have built companies that are inefficient, redundant and burdened by systems that do not communicate with one another."

Elitism and Misdirected Marketing

There are several parallels between the emergence of portable computing and the early days of personal transport. Motoring and its main benefit—freedom of movement—were the privileges of the rich while the market was limited to Benzes and Bugattis. Then Henry Ford came along to provide a low-cost means of personal transportation, and the rest is history.

Today, there are millions of people out there wanting the modern equivalent of a Model T portable computer. Instead, many portable office products are created for a financially and technically elitist market sector on mistaken premises about potential demand for portability. The consumers who seek status overkill in their automobiles are a very attractive and profitable market sector. But those in the computer industry who are tempted to devote disproportionate effort chasing those prepared to pay premium prices for the microprocessing equivalents of leather seats and turbocharged performance will miss out on the big opportunities. The demand—and long-term profits—lie in such applications as the notepad portables that one company is using to achieve 20 percent improvements overnight in the productivity of its delivery trucks and drivers.

While the portable office and other ''work to go'' concepts are exciting developments, there is a conflict between the actual needs of millions of us seeking work flexibility and what those developing and marketing portable office technology seek to impose on us for commercial reasons—or from just a plain misreading of the long-term opportunities in this field.

This reality is brought home repeatedly as I spend hours on the telephone answering questions about computer viruses. As a consultant director to the International Computer Virus Institute and author of books on viruses, I find that the periodic scares sparked by the latest virus infections let loose a deluge of inquiries.

Some questions come from big corporations with thousands of PCs, but most are from individual users or small businesses. Talking with these users drives home the point that the majority of people needing computer portability do not require great technical sophistication. Many do not even come close to being computer literate.

One consultant emphasizes that the lack of understanding of computer basics is far more widespread in the business community than most planners appreciate. ''That ignorance applies from chief executives right down to the newest recruit in the mail room—and especially to the chief executives,'' he says. ''Don't forget to explain what a keyboard is (and I'm only half kidding!).''

The demand for the portable office of the future is coming from the equivalent of the automotive mass market for the contemporary equivalent of the Model T—the Ford Taurus or the Toyota Corolla. Most of us want function with acceptable style and performance at the best possible price. Otherwise, we will hang onto what we have got, and the computer industry will experience the restraints that afflict the automobile industry in a replacement rather than a growth market.

The Practical, Affordable Portable

The portable office concept is not primarily about being able to take 40 megabytes of hard disk storage into the business class section of an airliner and running spreadsheets after dinner at 30,000 feet. It is about the freedom to get computing and other technological help to do an enormous variety of work when and where we please—word processing on the kitchen table at midnight, for example.

Portables are attracting entry-level computer users who are highly cost-sensitive and who need systems that are easy to operate. Attractive pricing, reliability, and ease of use are prime requirements. They are people like me—and perhaps like you, also—who don't need all the latest computing bells and whistles. Indeed, most of us don't even get close to using all the computing power that we have already.

At my desk I have a sophisticated word processor, a hard disk, a laser printer, and other contemporary features, but if I'm really honest, much of my work could still be done on my first CP/M system, with just twin disk drives and a daisywheel printer. Indeed, until a laptop came into my life, the old CP/M equipment used to be my portable office also, piled into the trunk of my car and carted from one working location to another.

Those computing needs are now more than met by the much improved popular entry-level integrated software packages and basic portable hardware that we will be examining in detail in later chapters. There is a lot you can do to save money and stretch the usefulness of existing equipment.

Many tasks that at first glance appear to require extensive memory and sophisticated hardware costing over $5,000 can be executed just as well for an outlay of under $2,000. You will learn how to stretch the capacity of cheaper equipment and how to get the best value for your money by taking advantage of those who have succumbed to commercial and peer pressures to trade up unnecessarily. There are some great used equipment buys around!

While time, the commodity of the future, is the driving force behind the portable office trend, excessive cost is having a negative braking effect. This precious time is not measured in nanoseconds of disk drive access or microprocessing speed—as the advertisements, and too much of the editorial, in the computer magazines would have us believe. Nor is portability strictly quantified by weight or size, cramming increasing amounts of high technology into ever-smaller pots.* What does count is

*An example of this was Apple being forced to cut the price of the first portable computer ''for the rest of us''—the Macintosh that weighs sixteen pounds will not fit on an aircraft table, has lead-acid batteries based on technology more than a hundred years old, and

flexibility and efficiency. The principles that make economic sense for those watching their personal budgets should apply also to shrewd corporate thinking, especially when it comes to cost-efficient mass application of portable computing.

Improvements in the Ease of Use

Those of us close to computing can easily get out of touch with the far larger population who find the hardware and software dauntingly difficult to use. The industry needs to listen more to the real computing needs of ordinary people and communicate better how to make best use of its products.

A significant step forward will be when someone produces a manual for a word processing program—the most universally used type of software—that is easy for anyone to understand. Better still will be when the software becomes so readily understandable that manuals are redundant. We are getting closer to that ideal. You can now chose software to carry out most business and personal tasks, with help menus and on-disk tutorials that enable you to take to the road without needing any hard copy documentation to clutter your mind and your baggage.

One of the most exciting prospects for the portable office is CD-ROM—*when* the suppliers get their acts together. Right now, prices are still too high and the quality and range of information available far too low.

But in Chapter 7 I look forward confidently to CD-ROM drives becoming standard features at a realistic price, so that this impressive technology is no longer self-limiting. About 200,000 systems in use by the end of the 1980s was only scratching the surface. But what can you expect with hardware prices three times what they should be, and with much of the limited software available being stale, unexciting, and overpriced?

The potential of CD-ROM is enormous. The ability to have over a quarter-of-a-million pages of text—the equivalent of over a hundred feet of books set out along a shelf—on just one compact disk makes portability an attractive reality for far more people.

If you are serious about putting database power into your portable computer, I offer some practical CD-ROM tips in Chapter 7.

---

originally cost upwards of $6,000. The Mac Portable, which came in for some snide remarks from the ''experts'' when it was first launched, actually matches the real computing needs of the vast majority of users in every respect but price. Apple reduced this by $1,000 in 1990, but we still pay too much for too little real progress in portability.

A Rewarding Adventure

Perhaps now you understand why at the beginning of this chapter I promised you an adventure in work and living. This is a fast-paced, action story. The first portable computer—the Osborne 1—appeared only in 1981. During the succeeding decade, developments progressed at an enormous rate, but they were only a foretaste of what is still to come. When *Personal Computing* asked its readers in 1990 to rank what systems they expected to have the most impact, laptop and notebook computers comfortably topped the list.

Soon you will find out why. As inspiration for the journey, consider what Dallas Vordahl of Spokane, Washington, wrote to *Micro Cornucopia* magazine. The fact that Dallas is handicapped may not be as significant as is the enterprising, creative way in which he has derived so much from a simple, low-cost system that is probably less powerful or costly than the one you have or are considering buying:

> I've used present computer technology to improve almost every aspect of my life: the way I work and play, the way I communicate and interact with other people, and the way I learn and think and challenge my mind.
>
> I'm forever lost in this computer adventure.

In this first chapter you have begun the adventure yourself by considering some of the portable office options that apply to your situation. In the following chapter, you begin to assess your actual computing needs, developing a specification for your personalized portable system.

2

How to Build a Portable Computer System

This chapter contains forms to help you identify your computing requirements and pair them with the hardware and software elements to build a system that will most exactly match your needs. Make notes on the forms and you will automatically build a customized specification by a process of selection, elimination, and compromise. It is the same process that a good consultant would follow.

If you have a portable computer already, examining the relationship between your computing needs and the various hardware and software configurations and services that are available will identify beneficial changes, additions, or substitutions.

You may be able to identify ways to extend the usefulness and reduce any deficiencies of your existing system without incurring significant expense. There are low-cost software options that can make existing hardware far more flexible and powerful. Eight programs on one disk, as described in Chapter 4, could run your business on a laptop. Or it may only be necessary to modify your working techniques to transform your productivity.

If you are new to computing and are contemplating your first purchases, pay particular attention to selecting the most appropriate software to avoid a succession of frustrating learning curves. A word processing spreadsheet or database program takes considerable time to learn and use proficiently—time largely wasted on programs that might require early replacement.

Conversely, if you are already familiar with particular software, think carefully whether the perhaps marginal benefits to be gained from switching to another program will justify the learning time involved. It is quite likely that the characteristics that frustrate you with your current word processing or accounting program have been fixed in a low-cost upgrade. Or there may be utility and other subsidiary programs that will make your existing software function better, including some that are virtually free of charge.

Even among the over 60 percent of personal computer users who are thinking of adding portability to their systems, there is the strong probability that expensive mistakes will be made. Adding portability is not just adding mobility to computing tasks. It is opening the opportunity to use a computer differently and more flexibly than before.

When drawing up specifications for your ideal portable computing system, let the dreams flow. We will turn them into reality later.

You might like to photocopy the forms, or place a bookmark or Post-It marker in the book to make the forms easy to find when you wish to add to or change the specifications. Also, I suggest that you read with a highlighting pen close at hand so you can emphasize information, points, or examples that relate to your particular computing needs. You can cross-reference these sections of the text by noting the page numbers at the relevant places on the forms.

The Tasks You Want Your Portable Computer to Do

The most important requirement for your system is that it efficiently perform the tasks you require of it. Make the system fit your needs. Do not compromise your requirements to accommodate any inadequacies in your hardware or software.

List on Form 1 the essential tasks for which you need computer assistance. Add optional functions you would like to have available but that are not so important. (Don't worry about price at this stage. There are ways to squeeze your computing needs into even a very limited budget.)

The Most Suitable Software to Do the Job

The most essential of the tools required to do those jobs listed in Form 1 is the software, or programming, that makes the machinery work. There are two main kinds of software: operating and applications programs.

Form 1. Tasks.

	Essential	Optional	Proficiency Needed
Word Processing			
Spreadsheets			
Personal Information Management			
Databases			
Accounting, Personal Finances			
Communications			
Graphic Design			
Desktop Publishing			
Education/Training			
Games			
Others			

Operating System Software

Nearly all portable computers use DOS—short for Disk Operating System—to control the computer's basic functions. You should ensure that your portable runs a form of DOS that is fully IBM-compatible. There are a handful of Macintosh and compatible portables that use Apple's system, generally offering less computing power for the money than similarly priced high-end portables using the more powerful microprocessor chips that run DOS and the new OS/2 operating system and Windows.

OS/2 is a more sophisticated successor to DOS, with the ability to do multitasking (that is, it can run several programs at the same time) and generally perform more efficiently in terms of speed and processing capacity. Another big attraction of OS/2 is that it will run Presentation Manager, a program which, like Windows, brings into the IBM-compatible world the multiple windows that split the screen to allow you to see and work in other programs (or other parts of the same program), together with friendly icons and other graphic interfaces of the type that have made the Macintosh so popular for those who put a premium on ease of use.

However, even the older and more basic desktop PCs and the lower-priced portables that use earlier generations of microprocessors can give you some of these features. You do need an upper-range portable to run OS/2, but far cheaper midrange laptops will run Microsoft Windows interfaces and graphics, which offer many of the same features in the DOS environment. Even the lower-priced laptops can perform competently with programs that offer many Windows-like features, including split screens, pull-down menus, and other ease-of-use attractions.

New DOS programs are being written all the time, and despite the commercial and peer pressures to keep on top of computing technology, your choice of software and the hardware with which to use it should be governed by what you really need. There have to be compelling reasons to buy a powerful machine for Windows and OS/2 when a far less expensive one will do the job.

The ability to transfer data and programs freely between your desktop system and your portable will influence both your software and your hardware choices, including the operating system you take on the road.

Another factor will be whether you need the ability to do graphics. Many users feel that the Macintosh system is still superior for graphics, in both its desktop and portable versions. In fact, DOS now has a wide range of excellent graphics programs that will run on portables.

A big Macintosh advantage is that all applications programs—the software that actually carries out the different tasks—run in the same way on the Macintosh System. Most Macintosh users never even give a second thought to their operating system. They use their computers productively without needing to learn much about how they function.

In contrast, you will not use a DOS system for long before you will need to make at least some effort to understand the apparently complex instructions required to format or copy disks, manage your files, and carry out other housekeeping chores. DOS is difficult to learn and to use, but not seriously so for the very limited numbers of commands that most users need.

DOS has—and always will have for the foreseeable future—a vast number of programs in its operating environment. There are tens of thousands of DOS system applications, and more are being written all the time. Many are free, or cost only nominal amounts. You can get them from bulletin boards or direct from mail order libraries. You try them out and only pay a small fee to register as a user if you find that you like them. There are far fewer programs for the Macintosh environment and they tend to be more expensive.

All in all, despite its defects, DOS has to be the first choice for portable computers at this time. It will never be outdated to the point of uselessness, just as my first portable typewriter still functions well after nearly forty years.

But the Macintosh System may have particular attractions for you, so don't dismiss it yet. There are alternatives to Apple's own Macintosh Portable, or ways of making desktop Macs into very functional mobile computers. Also, it is getting much easier, with the new software available, to move your data and other files between Macs and DOS computers, so you need not be trapped in one operating system or the other. While a Macintosh computer may not directly run programs or files created on a DOS portable, or the other way round, there are now very good programs that will allow you to transfer data between the systems.

That makes feasible an often overlooked option for Macintosh enthusiasts. Stay with your familiar—and expensive—Macintosh desktop system and use a portable from the far wider—and less costly—choice of DOS machines. Macintosh devotees will find that the DOS environment is nowhere near as hostile to them as it used to be. If you are familiar with integrated, user-friendly software such as Microsoft Works, you will find it is ideal for work-to-go situations, and you will soon learn to function as efficiently on your DOS portable as you do on your Macintosh in the office.

If you think you may need to use OS/2, or the XENIX or UNIX

operating systems, which have specific advantages over DOS, note this on the forms for both hardware and software because it will influence your choices. There are higher-level portables that will cope with all four systems.

If you are on a really tight budget and do not need maximum portability, the first mass-market personal computer operating system called CP/M (Control Program for Microprocessors) can get you going very cheaply. Some transportables using CP/M were produced in the early 1980s. They, and the CP/M desktop systems, can be picked up for a song now. I've seen Osborne transportables with lots of life left in them going for under $100. And there are still enough enthusiasts for the system around to ensure sources of software.

CP/M is outdated and restricts your selection of new programs or your ability to interface with other computers. Nevertheless, I wrote millions of words on a CP/M Exidy Sorcerer system to raise five children, running Spellbinder as a word processor. If I fall on hard times, I would not be too concerned about going back to that system to keep the wolf from the door!

There are thousands of people around the world doing sophisticated computing with CP/M, pushing their equipment far beyond the usage that many of us ask of our shiny new high-powered DOS and OS/2 systems. It is not too difficult to move data files created with CP/M into the DOS environment, or vice versa. It can be easier than converting Macintosh files to run on a DOS system, but even that is not very difficult.

Incidentally, check if your operating system is included in the price of the computer. If not, it's like having a car without the ignition key—unless, of course, you have a recent copy of DOS already. Some portables have DOS built in, on a special microprocessor chip. This is a great idea for efficiency but it limits your ability to upgrade later as newer versions of DOS are released.

Applications Software

Ninety percent of portable computer users can do many of their computing tasks with just one software package costing under $100. The integrated software packages that combine the most needed applications programs are superb. They are comparatively easy to use, do not demand a hard disk so they will run on a basic portable, and are very efficient in the way that they function. They enable you to combine and move easily between the main computing tasks for organizing your personal affairs and those of a small business or professional enterprise.

Integrated software still tends to be regarded as entry level, cheap, and consequently not sophisticated. This is a myth. Betterworking Eight in One, Microsoft Works, or PFS: First Choice integrated packages at around $100 are not the cut-rate low-grade choice, but the best way to go for the great majority of personal computer users. They have particular plusses for portable systems.

We will look at software alternatives in more detail in Chapter 4. In the meantime, I have entered these integrated software programs on Form 2 and urge you not to strike them out until you are convinced you have found better ways to process words, do accounts, write spreadsheets, create databases, and communicate via a modem.

Note also for the different applications the level of sophistication or capacity you are likely to require: basic, average, or advanced. The integrated software packages cover both average and many advanced needs, as will basic hardware without a hard disk if you are not in a great hurry and don't mind some disk swapping.

Form 2.   Software.

OPERATING SYSTEM:	Choice
MS-DOS, PC-DOS (list version no.) OS/2	
Macintosh	
Unix, Xenix, or Other	

APPLICATIONS AND UTILITIES

UTILITY PROGRAMS	Level of Performance Required			Choice
	Basic	Average	Advanced	
Collection (e.g. PC Tools)				
Battery Monitor				
Disk/File Management				
Diagnostic/Recovery				
Desktop Tools				
Security/Anti-Virus				
Others:				

APPLICATIONS AND UTILITIES

APPLICATIONS PROGRAMS	Level of Performance Required			Choice
	Basic	Average	Advanced	
Integrated Package: eg. Works, First Choice, Eight-in-One, etc.				
Word Processing				
Spreadsheet				
Database				
Personal Information Management (Contracts, Agenda, Personal Finances, etc.)				
Accounting/Financial				
Business				
Communications				
Graphics and Design				
Desktop Publishing				
Presentations				
Traveler's Specials				
Education/Training				
Recreational/Games				
Others:				

The Best Hardware for Your Purposes

The Computer

There are numerous choices within each of the main categories of hardware available, and you may well find as you fine-tune your tasks and software forms that your preferred hardware package turns out not to be what you first suspected.

You may conclude that it makes sense to get two portable systems that will work well together rather than one that is capable of doing everything. Not only may this be a more economical choice but it can also give you greater flexibility in how and where you do your computing. Wayne Barnes, who manages catalog sales for Traveling Software, the largest mail order specialists in the field, says that many businesspeople are now using pocket organizers or pocket or notebook computers to maintain their agendas, store contact names, and keep other essential data when they are on trips. The heavier and bulkier laptop goes along only when there is serious computing work to be done.

Form 3 has the basic hardware categories. Even if you hate the tiny keys and minute screens of the pocket or notebook systems, do not strike them off your list until you have given them a fair evaluation. Chapter 5 shows how some of their shortcomings are minimized and their advantages maximized if they can be integrated into a work-to-go system that makes sense for you.

There is such confusion about these different categories of portable computers that from here on I will refer to the following five distinct classifications. These are similar to those developed by the consultant firm of Arthur D. Little, which has done so much to popularize the use of portables in business situations:

1. *Pocket Computer*—a unit that weighs less than 1 pound and measures no more than 4 × 9 inches, with a thickness of up to 1 inch.

2. *Notebook Computer*—Can go up to 7 pounds, with a maximum size slightly bigger than a standard letter sheet of paper—10 by 12 inches. Maximum thickness is 2 inches, so it will still go into a slim attaché or document case.

3. *Mobile Computer*—Weighs under 10 pounds and is able to run from its own batteries. This category excludes portables that are dependent on 110- or 220-volt AC electricity. The use of the term *mobile* clarifies the increasing confusion over the word *laptop,* which is used to describe machines of varying characteristics.

4. *Alternate Office Computer*—Weighs under 16 pounds, is battery-powered, has high-quality displays to EGA monitor or higher clarity, and has a hard disk. I include in this category also those portables dependent on AC electricity but which meet the other criteria. As we will see in Chapter 9, there are several ways a computer can be mobile and use AC power at the same time.

5. *Desktop Substitute*—A powerful central processing unit of at least 80286 level, with an EGA or higher resolution display and a hard disk. I suggest we include in this category also the lunchbox portable, even if it only has the processing power of the 8088 CPU found in PC and XT desktops. These portables tend to have spare internal space so they can be customized to particular applications or expanded to add memory, expansion boards, CD-ROM drives, and other powerful features.

Form 3. Hardware.

COMPUTER TYPE		
	Preferred	Alternative
Pocket		
Notebook		
Mobile		
Alternate Office		
Desktop Substitute		
PROCESSOR	Minimum	Preferred
Type: 8088, 8086, 80286, 80386SX, 80386, 80486, Other		
Memory required		
Disk Type: e.g., Internal and external 3.25-inch (and 5.25-inch) double- or high-density floppy disk drives; internal and/or external fixed (hard) drives; smart cards and other media		
OTHER COMPONENTS		
Keyboard: size, layout		
Screen: size, type		
Internal Modem: baud rate		
Battery: type, life		
Service/Tech support		

The Printer

The most popular hardware after the computer itself is something to yield a "hard"—printed—copy of what you process. There is a limited choice of types of printers that are truly portable, and you may decide that you don't need one at all at this time. For example, even journalists and full-time professional writers may well not need to take a printer when they travel because they transmit their work by telephone or their deadlines permit them to produce the hard copy on their return to their desks.

Portable printers use versions of dot matrix, ink jet, or thermal technology to put the image on the paper. Those methods are rapidly being overtaken by laser or pseudo-laser technology for desktop systems. That means that if you buy a portable printer, it will probably cost significantly more to produce an inferior result compared to what is becoming standard for PC output.

When filling in Form 4, question whether you need to print hard copies that are not of the best quality, and whether your printing requirements are worth the premium for maximum portability. Unless you need to take a printer with you when you fly, it might be cheaper and produce better results to carry a small dot matrix or daisywheel printer in the trunk of your car or locate one where you will be working.

Printers are tough devices that travel well and draw little power, so can be run from a car battery through a converter if mains electricity is not available. The types made obsolete because they have been replaced by lasers can be very cheap. Indeed, you may have a dot matrix or older laser

Form 4.   Printers.

	Performance Required		
	Basic	Average	Advanced
Graphics			
Text Print Quality			
Speed			
Single Sheet, Continuous Form Feed			
Color			
Fonts Required			

printer with plenty of life left in it that is no longer needed for your desktop system. Companies replacing old printers might also consider their portable-computer users and out-workers before junking or accepting nominal trade-in allowances for dot matrix or daisywheel printers that could support portable computing operations.

Your Other Portable Computing Needs

Form 5 is the miscellaneous spec sheet for listing other hardware and services that you might need to complete your ideal system.

External modems, for example, come in all shapes, sizes, and performance ratings. Go unprepared into the store and in no time you can be seduced by the power of the latest 2400- or even a 9600-baud modem, which in theory is the fastest, most efficient device. But just as a Porsche is no match for a Jeep on journeys to remote places, too much sophistication in a modem may not be cost-effective and may create practical problems.

So don't make your modem choice automatically the fastest and most advanced technology you can afford, especially if you will need it on international trips or in places in the United States where telecommunications transmissions may not be the best.

Fax equipment needs to be considered carefully, too. You may need to send and receive faxes wherever you are, but can do that without buying a fax machine that hinders your mobility. Here is one area where you or your organization can save money and also contribute to your efficiency on the road.

Your portable computer, possibly in conjunction with your printer if you need hard copies, may provide most of the faxing capabilities you need. They can be turned economically into a high-quality, full-function fax. After reading Chapter 8, you will be better able to list your modem and fax requirements.

Cellular telephones, copiers, and other miscellaneous equipment for the portable office are highly variable needs. A copier is not necessarily the most efficient, most portable, and least expensive way of making copies when you are away from the office. You will find on Form 5 that copier options are linked with scanners because the cheapest and best way of copying on the road often is to scan into your computer the documents, books, or whatever you wish to duplicate. Then you can print out the copies—or fax them, without printing hard copies first. This saves time, telephone, courier, and other costs, and may enable you to transmit both text documents and graphics faster and to a higher quality.

Form 5. Accessories.

	Specification Required
External or Internal Modem	
Portable Fax or Computer Fax Card	
Cellular Phone	
Copier and/or Scanner	
Carrying Case	
Connectors, Adapters	
Portable Workstation	
Other	

Getting It Together

Having assembled the elements of your ideal portable computing system, how are you going to move it from place to place? These items are also covered on Form 5.

When I bought my second laptop, the salesman convinced me to take the manufacturer's customized shoulder bag that was designed to hold everything. The shoulder bag is tough and will hold most of my system components, but it was also very expensive and not particularly practical.

The R&D budget for my laptop and portable printer must have been used up by the time a designer got around to thinking about the converter or adapter required to run the units off the mains or to recharge their batteries. These elements seem to have been put together by the neighborhood blacksmith; they are heavy and bulky, with tangles of wires.

Consequently, the adapters and the printer almost always go in my checked baggage on flights. But there is still enough equipment to go into the shoulder bag from the manufacturers of my laptop to wreck my muscles and joints or crumple my papers when used as a carry-on. My chiropractor tells all his patients who fly frequently with portable computers to try to put them on wheels, on the well-proven theory that connecting flights always depart from the boarding gate farthest from where you arrive.

Some portables need special bags. Others fit best into briefcases. For some purposes, a hard case with a protective, shock-absorbent interior is essential. Some of the larger portables come very close to being too bulky for carry-on baggage requirements and so special consideration is needed for the case.

You may mainly use your portable system in hotel bedrooms, in your car, or slung around your neck as you walk from place to place. In Chapter 10 there are suggestions for setting up portable workstations, and these should be included on Form 5.

This chapter has provided the framework for making major decisions about your portable system. The chapters that follow contain the specifics to enable you to build on that framework. Next is "Software Selections," a two-chapter section on choosing the best software, the first, most important stage of that building process.

Part One
Software Selections

Selecting software for portable computing is not simply a matter of using desktop programs on the road. Most portable systems do not have—nor do they usually need—the processing power many have come to expect from desktop systems. This is particularly the case for business applications, where many desktop systems are both a hardware and software overkill. Important points to consider include:

- The hard drive regarded as essential for desktop use should by no means be an automatic requirement for a portable. Hard drives are expensive, add weight, and can gobble up battery power. Whether or not your portable has a hard drive will be a major influence on your system selections.

- The screen will almost certainly not be as easy to read as a desktop monitor. The liquid crystal display (LCD) is slower to change, and some typefaces are far less legible. Programs designed to run in color assume a different personality when squeezed onto a small screen and dressed in a monochrome display.

- Programs designed to be used with a mouse or that rely on a numeric keypad or particular key combinations may become miserably slow and awkward on compressed portable keyboards that combine key functions.

■ While most laptops should run mouse or track ball and other point-and-shoot input devices, the cursor created by software designed for desktop applications may be very difficult to locate on an LCD screen. Operating a mouse can be awkward and impractical in many work-to-go situations. It's bad enough trying to fit a laptop onto an aircraft seat or balance it on your lap in the departure lounge. Finding a flat surface close at hand over which a mouse will roll properly can be well nigh impossible. So you may well find that software you are accustomed to controlling extensively with mouse commands, you will have to operate on the road from the keyboard.

Selecting software for a portable computer should depend on your needs, not be done to accommodate the inadequacies of your hardware. That is why you should start to build your ideal system from the software that best meets your needs. Only then focus on the hardware to run those programs.

Unfortunately, most people go about this software specification process backwards, running into problems and additional expense that could have been avoided.

Part One examines the different tasks for which most people use portable computers. These tasks, including word processing, spreadsheets, personal information management, and accounting, are matched to programs that work well on portables. It concludes with a series of helpful questions and answers on choosing practical and effective software for portables. Chapter 4 considers two other options: the multipurpose integrated software packages that combine functions; and customizing software to meet your work-to-go needs.

The range of software that works well—or that can be adapted to work well—on portable computers runs into thousands of programs. At the end of this section, you should have a sufficiently broad sampling to convince you that almost any need can be satisfied. If you do not find the software you want on the shelves of the nearest retail store, search the indexes, editorials, and advertisements of the computer magazines. Some are listed at the very end of Appendix F.

The catalogs of the software libraries that distribute disks of shareware and public-domain programs often contain real gems. For as little as three dollars per disk, you can try out shareware programs. If you like one, you can become a registered user for a reasonable fee that may bring documentation and a newer version of the program.

3

Software to Put Your Portable to Work

A computer is only as efficient a tool as the software running on it permits it to be. Once you have defined what tasks you need your portable system to perform, the next step is to identify the software programs that will put the computer to work.

Form 1 in Chapter 2 helps you to define the tasks. Form 2 identifies the most appropriate programs for your particular needs. Now we move on to fill in the gaps.

Remember that you can be much more ambitious than perhaps you thought previously in running many powerful programs on quite modest equipment. All you really need may fit on just one disk, or you can metaphorically pack your portable computing system so efficiently that your briefcase can contain a full-function office.

Here are the options—and some specific suggestions.

Word Processing

This the most popular portable-computer application by far, so your choice in software is wide and you should not follow the first advice you receive. People tend to develop a loyalty to their particular software and few users know all that is available. Seek out several opinions, read the reviews in magazines, and try out several options to get a sense of how they look, feel, and function on the portable system you will use.

Some publishers provide demonstration disks that make testing easier; others run regular in-store demonstrations. With shareware, you can buy a program for very little or download it from a bulletin board, give it a thorough evaluation, and only if you are satisfied pay a registration fee.

In the right combination, even basic hardware and software can enable you to prepare, store, edit, update, print, or distribute all kinds and sizes of documents electronically, with great efficiency. Spelling and grammar checkers and other writing aids such as a thesaurus can improve the quality of written work, while mail merge and other features can reduce the drudgery of repetition.

The word processors in the leading integrated packages are remarkably sophisticated and do most tasks efficiently. They also facilitate the movement of information among other applications in the same package, a feature which is particularly useful when communication by modem is involved or you need to combine your words with data from spreadsheets and databases.

If you have a favorite word processing program already, or you need to exchange or process documents between portable and static computer systems, choose integrated software for your portable incorporating a word processor that is related to or at least compatible with the one used in the office. The word processor in Microsoft Works is very similar to that in Microsoft Word 4.0 and 5.0, for example. First Choice and PFS: Professional Write are blood relatives.

Most word processing programs these days will convert text into the standard ASCII (American Standard Code for Information Exchange) characters, which can be read by most other word processors, but full compatibility is not always possible between systems and you will probably lose the formatting when you transfer text from one program to another.

Consider slimming and customizing a powerful word processing program to run efficiently on a portable (Chapter 4 explains how to do that.) Or switch to a different program specifically designed for portables. The latter choice is limited at present, but Traveling Software's LapWriter and Ski Soft's Eye Relief are both attractive options that can transform the tiny screen with their large character displays.

Spreadsheets, Databases, and Personal Information Managers

These are all programs that enable you to retain, process, manipulate, and evaluate information. I have grouped them in the same broad category of software because each has the potential to be a more useful tool when seen in context with the others. Some can even substitute for others. For example, a powerful personal information manager with lots of features may have all the data-storage capabilities that you need, and so make a separate database unnecessary.

Spreadsheets crunch numbers very efficiently and are particularly useful for forecasting, budgeting, planning, and monitoring activities. By using formulas, you can see automatically the impact that changes in one area of a business can have on others.

Databases represent a wide variety of programs that enable you to store all kinds of information in electronic form, so that they are easily processed, updated, or recalled.

The potential of databases that are truly portable is enormous. We now have the means to take vast quantities of information anywhere they might be useful. Also, now there are much more convenient and efficient ways of putting information into a database wherever it is most readily obtainable.

Check the integrated packages first; some have really powerful spreadsheet and database modules. Also, consider slimming down such favorites as Lotus 1-2-3, dBASE, and Agenda to function efficiently on a portable (see Chapter 4).

Personal information managers (PIMs) are marketed as a separate category of software, but they are another form of database. They can be powerful organizers of all the information you need to enhance your working life, together with the ability to analyze projects and create detailed project plans. Agenda and GrandView are examples of this type. Other PIMs are more modest in their capabilities or more specific in their functions. You may decide to use a low-cost portable notebook or pocket computer or electronic organizer as your most convenient medium for PIM (see Chapter 5), and a laptop for other work-to-go, swapping data between them.

Examine if your on-the-road PIM requirements might be best met by a flexible program that is free-form, particularly suited to a portable environment, and accepts input and yields output in a variety of ways; askSam is such a program that can establish order out of your worst information chaos.

If your need is primarily to control information about your business contacts—for example, if you are in sales—then there are comprehensive personal productivity packages that will do virtually everything except pay for the drinks. Maximizer is designed to run on either desktops or 640K twin-disk laptops. It organizes telephone and mail contacts, appointments, notes about each contact that you can input easily while on the phone or on the flight home, prepares and mail merges letters with names and addresses, calculates your own personal expenses, and has a host of other features.

Accounting and Personal Finances

There is software available to carry out virtually any financial data processing on a portable computer, whether it is to enable a high-powered team to analyze a complex takeover or to help you balance the household budget on the corner of the kitchen table.

Look first at whether your needs can be satisfied by an integrated package. Some of the popular programs can be used to run a small business, or the financial tasks of a division or department in a larger enterprise. With some creative thinking, these integrated programs can be applied to meet a wide range of accounting, cost control, budgeting, and other financial needs within the biggest organizations.

If the integrated packages are not powerful enough, you can get specialized accounting packages that will run on portables and cover job costs, invoicing, payroll, inventory, accounts receivable and payable, and general ledger.

The personal finance software that runs well on basic portables is now so competent that it may be enough to cope with the needs of a small business. Particularly worth checking out is Quicken. It is readily available for under $50, runs well on a laptop, and will transfer data to and from big brothers like Lotus 1-2-3 and Symphony for more detailed or complex processing.

Graphics and Presentation Programs

Graphics programs and portables used not to be comfortable bed-fellows; now they make much more practical partnerships. Consider particularly the potential of the new-generation presentation programs that you can run on a laptop. Use them to power a full-color, big screen presentation to a large audience, or across a desk in a one-on-one situation.

The hardware-software match is particularly important with graphics programs. For advanced needs, you will need a hard disk and a powerful system. But lower-cost portable systems can do amazing things these days. The limitations you might have thought inherent in a low-cost system are now being minimized by clever software. Consider programs like Magician, which runs on as basic a system as a laptop with a single floppy drive but is capable of creating video presentations, slide shows, and other presentation material combining graphics and text.

If your graphics needs are modest—such as generating conventional charts from spreadsheet data—some of the integrated packages are efficient and easy to use.

Desktop Publishing

The portable computer has an expanding role to play in this fast-growing activity. The business community has tended to place too much emphasis on power and complication in desktop publishing, giving it the perception of needing elaborate, static hardware to run complex software. Many people think the portable is limited to such publishing-related tasks as preparing and transmitting copy.

Although the desktop is still the best place to produce publications with demanding layouts that incorporate several different type styles and graphic devices, many publications can be produced on portables. Some of the most effective printed communications have only a limited range of fonts and are simply laid out, so they are well within the capabilities of a portable.

Portability takes the creation and production of desktop publishing off the desk and into the field. For speed and flexibility, the portable has many advantages. Consider programs like PFS: First Publisher for portable publishing, but remember that the leading word processing programs now have advanced features that generate attractive text in a wide variety of layouts blended with graphics. So you may not need a desktop publishing program at all.

Remember particularly that it is not always easy—or even preferable—to create combinations of text and visuals entirely with the computer. Publishing tasks that seem beyond the range of a modest portable become readily achievable if you are willing to use scissors and glue for final make-up.

Other Software Tools

Utilities

Utilities are the programs that help you use the computer more efficiently. Some are particularly appropriate to portables, but they need to be selected carefully and taken on the road only if they play a really useful role. If you become a utilities pack rat, you will find that they can gobble up memory and some conflict with each other.

An essential utility I have already included on Form 2 is a program like Battery Watch, for around $40. Eventually all portables will have an accurate *battery monitoring system* built in.

Look at the utilities built into the integrated packages; they may have all you need. Otherwise, combination utility packages such as SideKick or PC Tools bring together the electronic equivalents of more business tools than your desk can accommodate. Notebook, calculator, clock, automatic telephone dialer, appointment scheduler, file protection and recovery facilities, mini-databases—all these and more can be found in the combination utility programs now available.

Among the special utilities available, consider those like GOfer, which will burrow among your files to find data, documents, or fragments of information. Lotus Magellan and ViewLink are examples of other utilities with powerful *file-finding* capabilities that can take over the housekeeping of your hard and floppy disks.

A *print spooler* like PrintRite is another attractive productivity aid for the portable user. Particularly if you are traveling without a printer, it is a great way to bring together into a compressed file all the documents you create that need to be printed or sent to your electronic mailbox. It enables you to preview the documents before they are printed, and acts as a convenient storage place during the printing process, returning use of your computer back to you while the printing continues.

Disk caches—of which there is a steadily increasing selection—are great utilities for the portable user. They may act as print spoolers while also speeding up other functions. Instead of having to access disk drives or the central processor of the computer all the time, a cache program copies frequently needed program instructions and current data into a special cache in RAM (the computer's short-term memory), where it can be reached quickly and easily. It's rather like keeping on your desk the files and equipment you need often, rather than away in a central filing room.

Of course, a frequent problem with portables is that you have plenty of disk capacity but not enough RAM, especially if you run several utilities. You can fool your computer with a program that turns a section of the hard disk into a fake RAM, thus freeing up more RAM space. This is cheaper than buying an extended memory board, and may be the only practical route with portables that have no means to increase RAM capacity. There is more about this in Chapter 7.

There are a number of *disk management and maintenance* utilities worth considering. These organize the contents of your hard disk so that the reading and writing are more efficient. They may make a marginal improvement in battery life as well. SpinRite is an example of a utility that goes further and helps combat the rigors of the road. It is particularly good at restoring bad sectors and tracks on the magnetic coating of a portable's hard disk, realigning them so that the chances of disk failure are reduced significantly.

If you want to get into the finer points of optimizing your system—or if you are developing applications for a significant number of corporate portables—there is a nifty utility that generates a record of every read and write operation. Among its attractions is that it is free—one of a wealth of helpful programs obtainable from PC MagNet, the *PC Magazine*'s on-line information service. Details of how to tap into this resource are in Appendix C.

Ken Skier's No-Squint Laptop Cursor increases the size of the cursor and, being able to vary the rate at which it flashes, makes it far easier to see on the screen of a portable, especially a liquid crystal display in adverse lighting conditions. (The reason that cursors look so fuzzy on LCD screens is that they are switched on and off rapidly and then, when they are moved at the same time, there is a succession of only partly completed displays.) The conventional cursor on a portable is blurred to the eye like the wings of a hummingbird. The SkiSoft program slows it down to a rate more like the flashing of a traffic signal, as well as makes the cursor bigger.

Transfers

The software that enables you to transfer files from one system to another has particular value for the portable computer user. You may need such a program if you have one of the newer computers without a conventional disk drive, or if your portable has removable disks that will not fit into the desktop system that is your other processing unit. But remember that if your transfer requirements are rare, it may be sufficient to couple the two systems via modem and telephone line, and let your communications software do the work. You do not need a public telephone line; you can make the transfer from extension to extension on a local network. Another option is to send your files to an electronic bulletin board or on-line service from one system and pick them up with the other.

However, specialist transfer software is more efficient and has other uses, also. The software is faster now and more versatile, while the cabling fits a wider range of hardware ports and, with some packages, is not as bulky as it used to be. (The stiff, heavy cabling to link peripherals to desktops is awkward stuff to carry around with you.)

The leaders in file-transfer packages have long been LapLink and Brooklyn Bridge. LapLink is particularly versatile and can transfer data at over 500,000 baud via the parallel ports. It can also double for various backup strategies with either a desktop or a portable, enabling you to select files by various parameters, such as those that are new or have been updated, and move them quickly from a hard disk to a diskette.

Don't consider the modern file-transfer packages as simply data-swapping devices to overcome the handicap of incompatible disk sizes. The software can be used constructively to increase the efficiency of both portable and desktop systems, and can be integrated into practical data protection backup strategies.

Another type of transfer program enables you to convert files from one word processing program to another, such as from WordPerfect to WordStar, or back again; the good programs preserve most of the formatting in the original. However, you should not need these specialist programs to transfer between portable and static systems if you have chosen word processing software with transferability in mind or you do not need to retain the formatting. Virtually all modern word processing software will convert into and accept ASCII text. Even if you lose the original formatting, it should not be a problem to restore it with template, style sheet, and search and replace tools.

Communications

We look at communications in general when we review the hardware modem options in Chapter 8. Some modems come with their own software packages. The universally popular Procomm is available as shareware or in its latest commercial form, and is a good candidate for the slimming treatment discussed in the next chapter. You can configure it to your needs and then copy the essential files to another disk for use when traveling.

Most of the integrated packages have competent communications programs, and these should be perfectly adequate for most uses, with the advantage that they are among the linked modules with which you process and store the data being transferred.

Traveler's Specials

There is a small but growing number of software programs specifically geared to the traveling portable user. PC Flight Guide is an invaluable resource on air travel information that enables you to plan and change schedules and to dig out a wealth of otherwise inaccessible information about routes, aircraft that fly them, and on-the-ground facilities including hotels, airport parking, conference centers, and car rentals.

You buy the basic program, then get monthly updates on disk. Although it is a bulky program that runs best on a hard disk, you can give it the slimming treatment to boil down what you need into a less demanding travel form.

Other traveler's software options include frequent-flyer flight logs, expense recordkeepers that meet IRS reporting requirements, and a whole range of flight planning, navigation, and aviation logbook programs for portable users with their own planes.

There are also some nifty traveler's aid programs starting to emerge, including a useful shareware one called Trip Planner that has a large capability for planning the best road routes between major centers in the United States.

A commercial program called Trip comes with a book of maps of U.S. states and cities. It sells for around $50 and generates itineraries, reinforced with road maps, between nearly 2,500 places in the United States.

Don't forget the airline booking and access to travel agents and other travel information available from the main on-line information services, including Genie, CompuServe, and Prodigy. Details are in Appendix C.

Remote Access

An important category of software being developed primarily for portable users is the remote access programs. The portable connects by modem to a desktop, mini, or even mainframe computer, not just to transmit data, but to use all the facilities of the base machine by controlling it from the portable's keyboard.

Software is loaded at both the base and the remote terminal, although inevitably there will be more cloning of the programs when one calls up the other, as has happened with transfer packages. The link between the two is just the normal telecommunications setup of a telephone line with a modem at each end. Most of these remote access programs offer password protection to reduce the risk of unauthorized use, but otherwise they vary considerably in both price and performance capabilities.

An example of a remote access application is an audit team collecting data on-site with a client and then transmitting it back to the base office. The same team can, from their laptops, control complex analysis and processing of the data they are collecting, right on through to drawing up balance sheets and even printing out a detailed report incorporating graphics.

Another example is someone on an extended business trip, using a lightweight laptop as a terminal to the base computer to maintain nearly normal office activities. In some highly computerized working environments, this person could function on the local area network and generate and respond to communications from colleagues or customers from Bangkok as efficiently as in the home office in Baltimore.

Games, Entertainment, and Other Good Things

Some programs for games run reasonably well on small portable screens; others have such good color graphics that on portables they are but a pale monochrome shadow of their real selves. Chess, of course, works well universally. The range of golf games is now enormous; you can practice on your laptop in your hotel room the course that you will actually play the next day. A golf instructional program to help improve your swing can be an amusing as well as practical traveling companion. Other software helps you keep track of your investments, stock price trends, horse racing, even over sixty lottery games around the country.

The stress of business travel is increasingly recognized as a serious problem, costing companies billions of dollars annually in lost productivity, poor decision making, and associated medical costs. An interesting genre of software particularly appropriate for portable users aids personal problem solving, creativity, self-understanding, and mental and physical well-being.

There are programs that work with audiotapes and biofeedback mouse input devices to help control stress. Some tackle that common business problem: difficulty in sleeping, especially when jet-lagged.

There is even a version of Eliza, the MIT computer therapist, that will run on almost any portable. After a particularly stressful day on the road, you can boot up Eliza and tell her all your problems. Now you can take not only your office with you on a business trip but your therapist, also!

Other such programs help the decision-making processes, combining the computer's logic with your own experience and intuition. These can be a help when important decisions need to be made while you are on the road and colleagues are not available to consult. (Some bulletin boards are good resources, either for actual programs or for recommendations.)

Cheaper, more robust portables are extending downward the use of computers for learning. Computer literacy is one of the most useful educational gifts to give to a young child, and there is an expanding range of software that helps you do this, or solve other scholastic problems, such as overcoming homework block. The range extends from preschool to college.

Basic Software Requirements

With the information so far, you should have some idea of your applications needs. But before moving ahead any further, here are some questions worth considering.

- *Will the software look good and function well on the portable's screen?* Screens play a far more important role when evaluating software for a portable than for a desktop system. Screens on portables are nearly all restrictive in one way or another. Try not to buy or accept any applications program until you see how it will look on *your* screen. Check for clarity, legibility, and general ease of use.

    Don't be put off by problems that may be easily solved. For example, a word processing package that is terrific in color on a desktop monitor at first came across on my laptop as tightly packed text in a flat monochrome. But experimenting with the display settings in the options menu and working always with double-spaced text transformed the appearance and increased the ease with which I could use the program.

    That double-spacing trick is ridiculously easy, but can be so effective. Opening up the text creates lots of space around it, making it far more attractive and easy to read. You reduce the amount of text displayed at any time, but the greater legibility might be preferable.

- *Will the software be a happy fit with your hardware?* All the popular integrated software packages (described in Chapter 4) support the dot matrix, daisywheel, ink jet, and laser printers likely to be linked to a portable. They also marry well with most displays, notably the color/graphics adapter (CGA) standard required by basic color monitors and most screens used in portables.

If you intend to use your software with a more sophisticated enhanced graphics adapter (EGA) or video graphics array (VGA) display, this is a key factor in selecting programs. To handle graphics and text in monochrome display on an IBM-compatible computer, get a program with Hercules Graphics Card compatibility. You almost certainly will be working in monochrome on portables for some years to come (until the technology and the pricing make color more available), so consider switching to a high-resolution monochrome desktop monitor also.

■ *Does the communications software support the Hayes standard command set for modem communication?* Only get a modem, and the software to control it, that will function to the industry-wide standard established by Hayes Microcomputer Products. This will ensure that you can access virtually any bulletin board, or exchange information most readily with other personal computer systems.

Hayes compatibility is to computerized communications as driving on the right-hand side of the road is to traffic in most countries. That analogy has particular relevance if you are communicating internationally or in certain specialized circumstances. Other countries may use different communications protocols, just as some of them drive on the left, not the right, side of the road. If you have a particular need for, say, the High-level Data Link Control (HDLC) international communications protocol established by the International Standards Organization, you may need special communications software. If you have large amounts of data or lengthy programs to transmit or receive, you need software and modems that will perform such tasks as compressing and decompressing data, or that can transmit at higher rates of 9,600 baud or more. There is more on such matters in Chapter 8.

■ *Is it fast and convenient to move into and out of the applications program? Is it easy to transfer files or data from one program to another?* Multitasking is a growing movement in personal computing. It is one of the main attractions of the OS/2 operating system and Microsoft Windows because they can run two or more applications programs at the same time. The better integrated software packages give you almost that facility at less cost and complexity, which is particularly useful in portable situations. At the least, you should be able to put a marker in one program to keep your place while you leave temporarily to perform a task in another program, ensuring that you can return to where you were with a minimum of problems.

■ *Do I need software that will run on hardware more powerful than the basic PCs and their clones—such as computers with 286, 386, or even 486 microprocessor chips and other features?* There is a steep price incline for portables with advanced and more powerful circuitry. You need to go that route if you use powerful or highly specialized software. But often even complex tasks can be done with programs that run quite happily on lower-end laptops.

A much-vaunted attribute of Windows, certain applications programs, and OS/2 is the ability to have two or more windows, or display splits, on the screen at the same time. If you are word processing on a long document, it can be useful to open a window from one section of text to look into another section, or to call up a reference. Otherwise you have to keep scrolling backwards and forwards, or closing down one program while you use another.

Windows really comes into its own on tasks like mail merge, when the text is in your word processing module and the list of prospects is in your database. To keep switching between the two without windows is very awkward. Or you are writing a report and keep needing to refer to information in the database, selecting some to incorporate into the report. Windows makes that much easier also. You really can work at your computer on an aircraft and have the equivalent of a filing cabinet accessible to you without the impossible clutter of the papers.

Some people find using windows confusing; others think they are invaluable. On some small portable screens, extra windows may be a mixed blessing. But even if you are not planning to use windows now, there could well be a time in the future when you will want them. The Microsoft Windows program needs a degree of computing power not found in many portables.

The good news is that you can enjoy many features similar to Windows without needing this memory-demanding program. There are applications programs that incorporate windowlike features but that do not need any other software and are slim enough to run comfortably on a portable. Microsoft Works is an integrated package with such features.

■ *Does a basic word processing program have enough features for serious work?* The most popular applications programs are word processors, so there has been enormous investment in improving them in the last few years. As a result, they have become more sophisticated and have acquired abilities that most people who process words never need. Chances are, your word processing requirements—even if you are a professional writer—can be accommodated on a single disk that is eminently suitable for work-to-go.

Some users place great importance on the WYSIWYG—What You See Is What You Get—factor. This means that the display on the screen matches the look of the printed output. Programs differ greatly in this respect. Some show very clearly how the printed page will look in terms of the type fonts, italics, boldface, line spacing, margins, and so on. Others give little indication of these variables but will simulate the printed output to varying degrees in a preview, or graphics, mode. Unfortunately, portable users cannot always use the graphics mode because it is complex, slows down operations, and consumes memory.

While all the good word processing software programs have acceptable on-screen displays, some are not as competent in providing accurate previews. If you use templates—standardized formats that either you create yourself or which come with the software, or as an option—WYSIWYG may no longer be relevant.

Dictionary and thesaurus features are a great help in word processing. Many people expect them on desktop systems, but they are less practical on portables, particularly those with only one floppy drive. The dictionary and thesaurus can consume a lot of memory, and may be the single factor that prevents the word processing software from fitting onto a disk. If you have the need to do spell checks on documents, select software with a dictionary of at least 75,000 words, to which you can add specialized words. The integrated software packages have this facility, and are able to check the spelling of a single word, a section of text, or an entire document.

Most of the integrated software packages will also, to varying degrees, search the text and automatically replace words. There are significant differences, however, in the maximum size of documents that can be handled.

Some programs require you to break long documents into sections, which may not be the disadvantage it seems. Very big files can become unwieldly, they tend to be more vulnerable to software bugs, and—like putting all your eggs in one basket—involve more risk than several small ones. I get particularly nervous working with large files on portables with imprecise low-battery warning systems, especially when the batteries are not functioning to their best. There may not be enough power left when you try to save a very big file, with the risk that some of the working copy gets lost or scrambled. Data on the file being overwritten can easily be damaged at the same time.

■ *Is the program flexible in moving data?* Data exchange is a crucial consideration for many users. When you create data of any kind, their value may depend on how easily you can move them around.

For example, you may need to move text in paragraphs or single sentences to different locations in a document, or you may want to move data out of the word processing application into a database, a graphics chart drawing program, or into some other special application. One of the inherent advantages of the better integrated packages is that you can move data around between the different modules of the same package comparatively easily.

■ *What particular requirements have you for database software?* The second most popular computer application is databases. Database needs among portable users differ greatly. Select software that generates a readable screen display on a portable and accommodates sufficient records. It can be sheer misery working with databases or spreadsheets on portables with inferior screen displays.

The program must be able to handle the amount of data you have, with fields (the separate elements of a database file) big enough for your purposes. The range of field size, the number of fields that can be stored in a record, and the number of records that can be contained in a file differ greatly among the databases in the integrated software packages.

Databases also vary considerably in their ability to search for information, to move that information around within the database, and to generate printouts. Compare the specifications with your portable needs, bearing in mind that you may want to transfer and process database information on other systems, notably desktops, and also exchange data with networks and mini and mainframe computers.

Although all the integrated software packages I suggest will transfer data directly between their database, spreadsheet, and word processing modules, some are limited in their capacity to import and export data externally. If you need to transfer data easily to and from pocket and notebook computers, select database software that can interface with these smaller portables.

■ *Does the spreadsheet have all the necessary functions?* Spreadsheet criteria include the ease with which you can work with the electronic equivalent of an oversized sheet of paper, reproduced on an under-sized screen. It can get very confusing and awkward trying to handle even a modest spreadsheet. That's when the ability to move rapidly from side to side or up and down, or to split the screen into windows showing two or more sections of the spreadsheet at the same time can be invaluable.

Hardly anyone buys a portable solely to do spreadsheets, so a major consideration is the ease with which the portable's software can import and export files from another system. Can the portable handle data in Lotus 1-2-3 or Microsoft's Excel, for example? All the recommended integrated software packages import and export files in ASCII, but otherwise are somewhat restricted in this respect.

Spreadsheets also differ in their functional features. If you need the ability to manipulate data or financial information in particular ways, chose a spreadsheet program that meets your needs in these as well as more obvious respects. Also useful when working on spreadsheets—especially in airplanes and other confined spaces—is a pop-up calculator utility.

You will, of course, need printed output that meets your requirements. Some software is much more flexible than others in producing an acceptable hard copy of a spreadsheet on a portable printer. Programs vary also in their ability to create graphs from spreadsheet data; some are just no good with graphics at all.

■ *What are the prime requirements for communications programs?* The software that controls your modem must be a good match to both your modem and to the system to which you will be communicating. Generally this is not a problem. While most modems have only one or two rates at which they will transfer data, most communications programs—including those in the integrated software packages—will blast the data back and forth at the most common 300-, 1,200-, 2,400-, and 9,600-bits-per-second rates. However, these programs are more limited in the file-transfer protocols that they support. They all have a form of Xmodem that enables most communications within the United States and internationally to function properly, but if you need Ymodem, Kermit, or other less usual requirements, add this to the communications line on Form 2.

Your communications software should, of course, support the Hayes standard I mentioned earlier in this chapter and have such basic facilities as a directory of numbers, from which you can dial automatically, and easy ways to send and receive files. Automatic dialing is not a luxury. If you use your communications software during peak times, the computer takes over the frustrating task of repeat calling until it gets a free line to your target bulletin board or system. Not all the integrated software packages have this feature, although you can script them to log-on automatically and so stream-line the procedures when you collect your electronic mail or call into a frequently visited bulletin board. (But do not put passwords into log-on procedures or serious security problems can arise if your portable and disks are lost or stolen.)

4

Integrated Packages and Streamlined Software

Software selection can be very difficult. Fortunately, integrated software meets the vast majority of portable business and personal systems with very little, if any, need for modification. The term has unfortunately come to be associated with low-cost, entry-level programming not of the required sophistication or capacity for serious business or personal use. That is nonsense. If possible, every portable computer system should run integrated commercial software to do the majority of business and personal tasks. It is cheap, reliable, easy to learn, well supported, flexible, and amazingly powerful.

The Many Benefits of Integrated Software

A big advantage for portable applications is that these integrated software packages have been fine-tuned to run quickly and smoothly with limited memory and processing power. They work much better on portables without hard disks than most complex, single-purpose applications. Some integrated software packages are so well compressed that they combine half a dozen advanced applications programs on just one microfloppy disk—and that can be a tremendous advantage in work-to-go situations. If you are in a car, on a plane or train, or in a host of other places not intended as working environments, having to change a disk can be very inconvenient. You drop it and it goes under the seat; there is nowhere to put the other disks safely, where you can reach them easily; your concentration is broken; and all kinds of other annoyances occur.

With an integrated software package all on one disk, you can switch in and out of word processing, databases, spreadsheets, communications, and other applications without missing a beat. A good demonstration of this is when you are transferring a sales report or an order via modem and telephone, and completing the interaction with head office may require a report from the word processor incorporating customer details from the database, calculations from the spreadsheet, and both uploading and downloading of files by means of the communications program.

A good integrated package enables even a novice to learn the functions quickly. If he or she encounters a snag, there is immediate help on-screen. The program may even contain sophisticated tutorials.

What About Custom Software?

If you are putting together a portable computing operation for a large organization, you might be inclined to commission custom software. You have specialized needs that have always required tailor-made software solutions—unique requirements not shared by other businesses. Perhaps your accounting, inventory control, or other procedures are highly specialized, or you require users to interact easily with the network or the corporate database.

That is fine in most computing operations, but portable applications must, by their very nature, be different. There are still few consultants or software engineers who have the experience or flair to tailor programs for specific laptop applications—and also make them fit naturally into the overall corporate operations.

The IRS field audit fiasco mentioned in Chapter 1 is an example of how vital it is to match portable systems to on-the-road situations. The software could have worked well on even quite modest desktops with hard drives, but when it was used in the laptops the IRS chose, agents found themselves constantly swapping disks, getting more and more infuriated, becoming hostile to the whole concept, and seeing themselves as less efficient than they were with pencils, paper, and pocket calculators.

Another consideration is that any software has bugs (errors in the coding) that prevent it from working as it should to varying degrees of severity. It takes time and extensive use to identify and eliminate those bugs. Well-proven off-the-shelf software has been produced with investments in time, money, and testing to make it as bug-free as possible. So if there is a ready-made program that will fit your corporate needs, make this the first option.

If necessary, you can use the standard programs as a base and tailor them to meet particular computing needs. This takes but a fraction of the time and cost involved in creating programming from scratch.

Many commercial programs can be customized easily. You can modify sophisticated and complex applications programs to fit on a single disk, configure them to speed data transfers by modem, eliminate the need for a mouse, set them up to get the best quality from a portable printer, and in many other ways fine-tune the software.

Templates are available or can be created to customize applications programs for business requirements. There are templates for databases and for word-processed text documents; for the forms required to fill in credit applications, product specifications, order details, invoices, statements, insurance applications; and for many more portable computing tasks. For example, templates can be used to speed cash flow when salespeople prepare invoices on their clients' premises when taking an order.

Beware of taking what might be complex accounting software from the office and trying to use it under adverse conditions on the road for a simple estimating or invoicing task. Either use an alternative, simpler program or customize, perhaps with the use of templates, just the elements of your main accounting package required to generate an invoice.

If you are not familiar with the principles of templates, it is worth learning more about them. They can be so useful in portable computing applications to increase productivity under what might be difficult working conditions.

Templates are, for example, an important element in the computing activities of many of the over 5 million users of dBASE software, who need to develop applications programming in the easiest, most efficient way. That is why templates are a major feature of dBASE IV.

They change the way we use applications programs, particularly word processing, databases, and spreadsheets. Templates make novices into programmers, while also enabling expert software engineers to work faster and more efficiently. They are extending the functionality of even modest portable computers. You can buy templates from independent software authors to add power and convenience to your application, turning it into the equivalent of customized programming without all the expense and problems.

Training and Support

The other major saving with off-the-shelf software is that it can dramatically reduce training and support requirements. Establishing a portable computing operation usually involves also extending the use of computers in an organization, with the training of staff one of the biggest challenges and expenses. Good commercial programs that run well on portables tend to have the best documentation, on-disk tutorials, and help facilities linked directly to the operations. Suppose a user gets stuck running a spell check or changing the field size of a spreadsheet. Being able to press a two-key combination to receive immediate on-screen instructions can save a company a lot of money and hassles. That is particularly the case when computers are used in the field, in a hotel room after normal office hours, or in other typical work-to-go situations.

Making the Choice

Performance and suitability for individual needs at a very attractive price are features of integrated software. This is a rapidly developing, highly competitive market with heavy discounting going on all the time. You may pay only 60 percent of the list price or find the software "bundled" with other offers. Microsoft Works, for example, has been given away with Toshiba laptops, while its main competitor, First Choice, has been sold at greatly reduced prices along with free copies of Quicken, one of the most proficient programs for managing personal and small business finances. DeskMate is pushed very hard by the Tandy Corporation (Radio Shack), and the integrated package is given away or heavily discounted when sold with Tandy hardware.

Works, First Choice, and Betterworking Eight in One should probably be the first three packages you consider. They are described below, along with some alternatives.

Microsoft Works

Works is probably the best system for most portable users. It has clear pull-down menus that look good in the limited gray scale of an average portable screen. The word processor, spreadsheet, database, and communications modules are well integrated so you can move data easily between them, and they function in a coordinated way. Its advanced use of windows enables you to see as many as eight files in any or all of the four functions at the same time.

A big help when traveling is that you can automate with macros many activities, such as accessing your electronic mail. The word processing is surprisingly powerful and very similar to Microsoft Word, the stand-alone word processing program sufficiently sophisticated to do much desktop publishing. So you can move documents easily between Works and Word, and adjust to each program with minimum difficulty.

There are also strong similarities between Works for the Macintosh and for IBM-PC compatibles, which is an advantage if you have to transfer data between those two operating systems.

Works has a really outstanding tutorial to help the novice learn the program. If you run into a problem, the summarized help instructions are only a keystroke away.

My first integrated package lacked this kind of tutorial and I made a round trip of thirty miles once a week for two months to attend lessons. It's far easier to have the teaching on a disk you can access any time—and the Works tutorial is a more efficient learning device than the average live instructor.

As Works has become more powerful, it has also become fatter. If you have only floppy drives, you may want to tailor it to your system. All the Works applications fit onto a single 720K floppy disk, leaving room for some data files if you omit the large tutorial, thesaurus, and spell checker. (Keep these on a separate disk for when you need them.)

I have taken a slightly different approach that works ideally on a twin-floppy portable. On one disk I have all the executable Works files I need plus the MS-DOS operating system, the mouse driver, and the spell checker. With just one disk, my computer boots up and does all the tasks I require, with the second drive free for data storage and no need to keep swapping disks. You can easily create such a customized disk by copying the DOS file onto it, using the /s command. Then copy the Works program files and the spell checker, if you need it, using the DOS "file copy" commands.

PFS: First Choice

My second choice—but a favorite for anyone who seeks ease of use and friendliness—is First Choice. It is very easy to learn, very friendly in its display and command structure, and surprisingly powerful in its later versions. (These expanded versions are becoming more sophisticated and may need the slim-down customizing treatment I described for Works.)

First Choice looks good on most portable screens and, like Works, has useful affinities to more powerful single-application programs from the same publisher. In this case, you can move smoothly to and from PFS: Professional Write and PFS: First Publisher. (The latter is a really neat desktop publishing program with a large clip art library. The program runs well even on lower-end portables. It is one of the few desktop programs suitable for portable situations because it has been specifically designed for use with dot matrix and ink jet printers.)

Betterworking Eight in One

Eight in One does not have as attractive a display on color monitors as some of its competitors. This is no handicap on the typical portable display. The program is fast to use with either keyboard or mouse and has great word processing and large spreadsheet capacity, but moving between applications is not very slick.

Betterworking Eight in One runs well on just two floppy drives and is amazingly comprehensive for a very low price. You may find it discounted to under $50. It comes complete with a number of utilities, including an alarm and an international clock, which gives the time in sixteen different cities.

Integrated 7 Advanced

If you are a confirmed Lotus 1-2-3 user, then the Integrated 7 Advanced package's spreadsheet offers a familiar environment and it has good graphics capabilities. The limitations of its other applications have prevented it from capturing many sales from its more attractive competitors.

Q&A

Q&A is an integrated package with limited applications but unique features concentrated in powerful word processing and database applications. It is expensive, but should be considered first for portable use by the many businesspeople already familiar with the Q&A Write word processing software as well as anyone who needs a powerful database. There is an OS/2 as well as a standard DOS version.

DeskMate

Tandy Corporation's DeskMate will appeal to users familiar with this software family's attractive pictorial interface. It is easy to use, has lots of utility programs packed in along with its prime applications, and is attractively priced. While not as powerful or sophisticated as Works, it offers in one package enough productivity enhancers to meet the needs of many people.

WordPerfect Executive

If you are familiar and happy with WordPerfect as your word processing software, then the obvious integrated package for you is WordPerfect Executive.

This program slims down the powerful word processing module to run on a microfloppy and adds a number of utilities specifically suited to portable users, including an agenda, expense report, and itinerary generators. In fact, it is a condensed version of the most relevant functions from WordPerfect, PlanPerfect, and WordPerfect Executive that a businessperson is most likely to need on the road.

The snags, as this book goes to press, include a weak database and the absence of graphics and communications capabilities. It is also more expensive—usually by over $200—than integrated packages that offer more, although no others can so well satisfy the work-and-go needs of WordPerfect addicts.

AlphaWorks

AlphaWorks has a very powerful and flexible database and spreadsheet, coupled with the ability to juggle a large number of open files. If you are a power user taking to the road with at least 512K RAM and two floppy drives (but preferably with a hard disk and a megabyte of RAM), this package is well worth your consideration. (Framework III is another option if you have plenty of portable processing power—and money.)

Because user requirements vary so much, and the integrated packages are being improved all the time, it is not possible to suggest a universal best buy. They are all worth a close look to find out which best matches your particular needs. Ironically, the updates are not always as attractive to the portable user if they add on features that make the program bulky. You may prefer to get an earlier version, rather than be forced to customize it to fit your on-the-road system, or have to remove any active utilities competing for memory space.

Of course, despite their attractions, integrated software packages may not be the best choice for you. There are many other options, including the ability to shrink powerful stand-alone applications programs so that they travel better. We look at those choices next.

Incredible Shrinking Software

Despite their many advantages, integrated software packages may not be right for you. You may prefer the applications you use in the office. The good news is that most of these powerhouses can be shrunk to make them more suitable for portable computers. Even many versions that call for a hard drive can be put through an electronic crash diet that makes them lean enough to fit on a single microfloppy disk.

Even if your portable has a hard disk, it can be worth slimming down the applications programs and modifying some of their activities to create extra space on your disk for utilities and data; slimming software may also speed up operations and reduce power consumption as added bonuses.

There are exceptions to every rule, and some programs cannot be reduced without making them impossible to use. But those usually are the programs that would not normally run well on portable equipment anyway.

For example, computer-aided design (CAD) and sophisticated graphics and presentation programs need considerable memory and processing power, and a high-quality monitor. A standard desktop system may not run them, let alone a typical portable. As a general rule, these programs cannot be trimmed for travel. (Fortunately, there are slim but efficient graphics programs that *will* run on an average portable. You can still capture visual creativity on the road, or use your portable when pictures are more effective than words.)

Processing words is the prime portable computing activity: probably over 50 percent of the time laptops are in use, they are running word processing programs. Fortunately, the high-power desktop software is among the easiest to customize for portable applications. But spreadsheets, databases, utilities, communications programs—even games and DOS itself—can be squashed to varying degrees.

How to Reduce the Software

In some cases, the easiest route to a slimmer program is to install a second copy of the program on the hard disk of a desktop system and then to customize that copy to the point that you can transfer it to a floppy disk (or to the hard disk or other storage device used by your portable).

Let's look at how to slim down a high-level word processing program such as Microsoft Word 5, WordPerfect 5.0, or WordStar Professional 5.0. (A particularly attractive operation would be to squeeze SkiSoft's Eye Relief, with its oversized screen characters, so it will run well on low-powered portables with undersized screens. If inadequate screen and limited memory are the main reasons you want to replace your present portable, you will find the following tips offer fast, economical, and practical solutions.)

Eliminate the Documentation. Do not be put off if the word processor came in a big box with bulky manuals and maybe eight or more floppy disks. It doesn't take long to become familiar with the features you are likely to need on the road, and the manuals can stay at home.

If you must have hard-copy help with you, there are compact ready-reference manuals, keyboard templates, and reference cards for most popular software available from third-party suppliers by mail order or through retail outlets such as Egghead. They cost under $20—some under $10—and will fit into any laptop carrying case. If there is not one for your program, get a blank template and fill in the details yourself; it is a great way of learning the key commands.

Many of the programs come with plastic templates to identify function keys and other keyboard actions. These templates and other quick-reference devices are usually designed for standard desktop keyboards, but some trimming with scissors can tailor them to most portables. I use my portable almost entirely for word processing, so I have cut up the Microsoft Word 5 template and used its adhesive backing to fit onto the plastic casing of my Zenith laptop. An alternative is to use adhesive-backed Velcro tabs, so that the ready reference guides can be attached and removed easily.

Delete the Surplus Files. Having got rid of the manuals, you can start salami-slicing the software itself. Working from copies of the original disks, first eliminate all surplus documentation from the slimmed-down version you are creating. Go through the README and .DOC files, extracting the information you really need and deleting these files from your customized copy. (Incidentally, as portable computing increases, some software publishers are giving instructions on reducing the memory requirements of their programs so they can be taken on the road or run on lower-powered desktops. This information may be in the README files, pending its transfer to the main manual, when the next edition is printed.)

Delete the Tutorials and Helps. Next, start deleting the tutorials and help files, which can take up a lot of space. An alternative is to copy them onto a special disk that you can take along if needed. You may find it convenient to compile a disk devoted exclusively to tutorials and help files—a miniature library of manuals for reference on the road. It might, in some circumstances, be worth transferring an entire manual onto a disk. The time and effort might be difficult for an individual user to justify, but could make sense in a corporation where many portables are involved. There are, of course, copyright considerations.

Many tutorials and help features come on separate disks, in which case you simply copy those you need directly onto a microfloppy or edit them to take up minimum space on your portable's hard disk. Shareware and public-domain software programs that usually have their basic documentation on disk are, in this respect, particularly easy to customize.

Delete Extraneous Printer Files. The customized disk is now looking much trimmer, but you can reduce its size further without impacting on its ability to function.

The proliferation of printers and the increasing sophistication of software have resulted in word processing programs coming with even bigger printer driver files and font utilities. You will probably need to specify only one type of printer for your portable computing tasks and only one or two different fonts. Maybe you don't need to make a hard copy at all when you are traveling. So all those surplus printer and font files can be dumped.

Review and Delete Other Nonessential Files. The installation procedure is another section of surplus programming that can be jettisoned. Free the disk space taken up asking you questions and processing your answers as you configure the program to run on your system. Once you have your application set up for your particular laptop with its type of screen, disk drives, ports, printer, etc., the installation files can be eliminated from your slimmed-down version.

More excess baggage may be found in files running functions you never use for work-to-go. There may be overlays, style sheets, graphics facilities, layout previews, and other functions that you use only when preparing documents for printing in the office. If you normally transfer your data from the portable to a desktop, then there is no point having that programming in your portable.

Big space savings can be achieved by eliminating the spell checker and dictionary, the thesaurus, and certain library and formatting features.

Do a Test-Run and Make a Backup Copy. Of course, after you have done all this cutting and copying of an applications program's files, give the customized disk a test-run to ensure it functions properly before venturing forth with it as your only resource. Also, make at least one back-up copy of that customized copy in case the original is lost or damaged.

With some programs, the slimming-down process may be as easy as copying only the essential executable files. Other programs may require some exploration of the disk directories and the manual. The degree to which you trim and customize reflects the trade-off between your desire to conserve memory and your need to retain features.

Special Slim Word Processors

Special word processing software for portables is now available that accommodates the dictionary and virtually everything else on just one disk. XyWrite and LapWriter are two examples. Another is a descendant of the popular shareware program PC-Write that is simple, easy to learn, and requires only one floppy and 356K RAM—or 384K to run with the spelling checker. PC-Write Lite is gaining ground among students using portables. A fully registered package costs under $80; it's under $50 for just the manual and disk, and only $12 for a set of the 5.25- and 3.5-inch disks to get it running on both desktop and laptop computers.

Figure 4-1 lists the features of this slimmed-down shareware to act as a benchmark for what a practical, on-the-road word processor can provide.

Other Possibilities

Even compact word processing programs that use as little as 150K may, with advantage, be reduced in a traveling version to create more space for utilities or data storage. After all, you may want the convenience of starting and running both DOS and your word processing from a single disk with space left to store data on it. Your program manual should give instructions for this simple procedure; if not, contact the manufacturer's technical support service or a user group.

You can slice some fat out of DOS as well, if you feel competent to do so. There are a lot of DOS files that even experienced users never need. Making DOS lose weight depends on the version you are using. Some likely categories for treatment are the files needed only for certain device drivers, for hard disks if you do not have one in your portable, for program creation and debugging, and similar activities.

Figure 4-1.   PC-Write Lite feature list.

KEYBOARD, CURSOR MOVEMENT:
- Use function keys or Lotus-style menus
- Many Wordstar control keys also supported
- Record, play back text phrases or commands
- Accent key for scientific, foreign characters
- Single, double line drawing keys, box frame
- Spaces and hyphens can be normal or hard
- Sticky shift for one-finger use, visual beeps
- Supports PS/2, PCjr, Tandy 1000 keyboards
- Over 26 cursor movement and scroll keys
- Save your place with two bookmarks
- Display, jump to line in file or page number
- Many custom keyboard and display options

EDITING ACTIONS:
- Pushright (insert), overwrite typing modes
- Split screen to edit in two places or two files
- Left/right delete of character, word, line
- Mark both normal and box/rectangle blocks
- Highlights block/box to move, copy, delete
- Delete line, block, or box; undelete option
- Copy, append block/box to file or hold area
- Insert file or hold area at cursor, box insert
- Slide line or block left/right for exact layout
- Transpose left/right, upper/lower case
- Manual, wordwrap, automatic reformatting
- Convert tabs to spaces, fix line breaks
- Count letters, chars, words, word length
- Insert date in fixed or custom format
- Match () [] {} < > pairs, auto-indent lines
- Insert any byte, find or strip non-ASCII
- Edit control file to set defaults and options

SEARCH AND REPLACE:
- Search forward/back, from cursor or top
- Lower case matches upper case, accented
- Wild cards match alpha, non-alpha, line end
- Replace matches wild cards and upper case
- Replace once or repeat in file or block
- Enter search/replace text only if changed
- Un-replace; swap search and replace text

FONTS AND EFFECTS:
- Underline, bold, italic, sub/superscript, wide
- Pica/elite in draft/letter quality, compressed
- Assign fonts on character, line, or file basis
- Combine fonts, effects; display using color
- Most popular printers supported
- Easy to customize printer control files

MARGINS AND RULERS:
- Embed, edit, load, and search for ruler lines
- Ruler has shadow cursor, current margins
- Right margins: ragged, center, justify, flush
- Left: normal, indent, hanging, forced-left
- Tab, decimal tab stops, mini-rulers
- Temporary left, right, paragraph margins
- Force end of paragraph, protect table

HEADERS/FOOTERS, FOOTNOTES:
- Up to 8 lines in each header and footer
- Page number, date in header/footer
- Left, right, center, mixed header/footer text
- Footnotes to page end, or file as endnotes
- Set footnote spacing, footnote fence lines
- Automatic page and footnote numbering

PAGE LAYOUT:
- Easy menu handles all common formatting
- Format commands can be visible or hidden
- Multi-line spacing, lines-per-inch leading
- Page, body length; left, top, bottom margins
- Hard page breaks or repage for soft breaks
- Displays actual line and page breaks

PRINT COMMANDS:
- Print single sheet, fan-fold, multiple copies
- Print whole file, or range of page numbers
- Print file series to handle large documents
- Print control file customizes, sets options

FILE COMMANDS:
- File backup option on entry
- Fast file save, with automatic save on exit
- Auto-save or reminder, time or input trigger
- Switch, name, delete, copy files
- Quick switch and search among related files
- Select from directory at filename prompts
- Standard ASCII files, good for programs
- Reads non PC-Write files, Ctl-Z at end OK
- Files as big as DOS memory, splits if larger
- Standard DOS pathnames, PATH= names
- Reads SET LITE= for control file switching
- Run DOS with PC-Write Lite resident (shell)
- Converts files from Wordstar, to/from DCA
- Automatic file lock on networks

SPELLING CHECKER:
- Check last word typed, or whole document
- Option to check every word while typing
- Select correct word from suggestion list
- Suggestions fix common typing mistakes
- Word lists in memory for quick access
- 50,000 word master list has common names
- Custom user word list for additional words
- Can add user word list to master word list

DOCUMENTATION:
- Status line gives modes, line/page, filename
- Optional three reminder lines give options
- 45 on-line help screens, can be customized
- Friendly first screen menu for beginners
- Compact manual with DOS guide, tutorial

REQUIREMENTS:
- IBM PC, AT, PCjr, PS/2, or compatible
- 5.25 or 3.5 inch disk drive, DOS 2.0 or later
- Display: normal 25 line, 43 line EGA, others
- Req. 384 KB RAM (256 KB if no spell check)

Source: PC-Write Lite.

It may be tempting, after squeezing a lot of programming into a small space, to pack more software into any gaps on the disk that are left. But it is best to resist this temptation and keep your traveling word processing program disk for that one function, or only to add the DOS startup, mouse drives, and a caching facility. Most word processing programs need additional disk space for temporary storage of files being worked on; you need to leave plenty of room for this to avoid any risk of hanging up your work in progress and perhaps losing data.

Other applications programs can be slimmed down to fit portable applications, including spreadsheets such as Lotus 1-2-3. A tip from Toshiba's experts enables 1-2-3 to function well on a single-disk computer such as the T1000 by misleading the program into thinking there are two drives. You instruct Lotus to save files to drive B, which of course isn't there, but the program will not know that if you respond by removing the system disk and replacing it with the disk onto which you want to put data files. Another approach is to use a memory expansion card as hard RAM, creating a drive D for the Lotus system files and enabling the data files to be saved to drive A.

If you find it difficult to trim the latest version of a program to work on your portable, take a look at the previous version. You may not need all of the new version's bells and whistles that have made it grow to take up substantially more disk space.

Compression Programs

Another approach to slimming programs for a portable computer is to use special compression software that squeezes both applications programs and data files so they take up less disk space, then expands them back to normal size when you need them. This is most useful when you send or receive a lot of information by modem; you may be able to reduce expensive on-line time by 50 percent or more.

The compression programs work by taking out coding that doesn't do anything, but still occupies a lot of space and transmission time. The spaces between words and the blank lines between paragraphs in text files, or the unused space in spreadsheet files, are not electronic voids. They may have the same effect as if they were filled with characters. When a file is compressed, all those spaces are replaced by much shorter coding that records what space was there. The coding also enables the spaces to be restored when the file goes through a decompression process.

This principle works well with data files that usually have large amounts of unused space. Applications programs should be much tighter, so the gain from compressing may be too small to be worthwhile.

By clever use of a compression program on a portable system you can achieve many of the benefits of an additional disk drive or of using high-density 1.4 megabyte microfloppy disks instead of the 720K standard disks. Disk write and read times are reduced, which can save battery power, and you may cram twice as much data into the same space.

The universally used file-compression utilities are shareware programs called ARC and PKZIP. Another interesting program costing about $100 is Squish Plus, which incorporates password protection and can enhance the performance of portables by creating files that simulate separate disk drives (called "virtual disks") to hold the compressed files.

You can use these and the slim-down techniques singly or in combination to create your own customized, multifunction disks to meet your specific work-to-go needs in the most compact, convenient, and power-miserly way. Such a suite of individual programs will not interrelate and swap data as well as the integrated software program we examined at the beginning of the chapter, but that may not be an important consideration for you.

Part Two

Your Ideal Hardware Formula

Just one word dominates the assessment of hardware options for portable computing: *opportunity*.

Portability adds opportunity to computing—the opportunity both to work anywhere and to add the power of computing to tasks that cannot be brought to the place where a static system is located. Indeed, J. D. Hildebrand, editor of *Computer Language* and a guru of work-to-go technology, defines portable computing as "opportunity computing." To achieve the greatest opportunity to use a portable computer, you must strike a balance between performance, price, and size.

Hardware decisions may be viewed on this opportunity scale, with greatest portability—smaller size—at the low end, and maximum computing power, involving greater size and cost, at the other.

Agenda Notes Addresses	Small, spread-sheets	Simple word processing	Advanced word processing	Desktop publishing	Graphics Databases	Windows	CAD	OS/2
1	2	3	4	5	6	7	8	9	10

Maximum portability and opportunity to use
Least computing power required

Minimum portability
Most computing power required

Your needs will determine where on the scale your ideal hardware can be found. In comparing portable systems, you will find that the choices always represent trade-offs and compromises.

The computer industry's marketing is oriented toward persuading buyers that they need to be toward the right end of the scale, where profit margins are greatest. In fact, over 80 percent of portable users could strike the best compromise between power and opportunity at around 1 to 3 points on the scale; few need to go over 5. Opportunity computing may be maximized by having pocket or notebook hardware at, say, the 1–2 level, augmented when required by a laptop coming in at around 3–6.

Bear in mind that some portability-opportunity relationships are apparent on this scale, but the comparisons are not as clear-cut as they might seem. Often you can tailor the features that you value most as you fine-tune your selection of hardware and software (particularly using the techniques described in Chapter 4 to achieve greater software power in portable equipment).

Assessing your hardware options is made more difficult because you must completely reverse your perceptions of size in relationship to both power and price that have characterized desktop computing's macho machines in imposing tower cases.

The premium prices of high-powered portables are instead linked to getting the greatest performance in the smallest package.

When considering computing hardware, seek the point where portability and opportunity start to diverge. What you gain in portability trades off in lower performance that limits your opportunity to do computing tasks. Then the decisions become even more based on personal need.

Much research and development are aimed at bringing more power to the most portable computers, which enables them to be priced more profitably and to extend their market. The other main effort is toward lowering the price in key sectors to stimulate a mass market. However, continued effort will go into premium portables packed with features for the executive market, where profit margins are easier to maintain because buyers are less cost-sensitive.

Portable computing can create many opportunities, especially if you optimize your hardware purchases. Chapter 5 discusses the portable computer options, Chapter 6 examines screens and keyboards, Chapter 7 reviews the power and storage choices, and Chapter 8 looks at peripherals. With this information you should be on your way to finding your ideal hardware formula for your portable office.

5

The Forms and Functions of Portable Units

The power and performance needed for work-to-go activities come in many different forms, from simple wrist units to heavy 386 mobile offices weighing over twenty pounds. As portable computing technology develops, size and shape will increasingly bear less relationship to power, although there will still be serious compromises made to pack high performance into small containers.

Price remains closely related to performance and compactness, but less so all the time: Prices fall as competition and market volumes increase. Your portable computing objectives may be most cost-efficiently achieved by combining systems, as in buying two sets of complementary hardware, instead of trying to find all the features you want in a single computer. For example, the limited function computer you wear on your wrist or slip into your pocket can become a very powerful personal productivity tool when it is integrated with other elements of your system rather than treated as a stand-alone unit.

Pocket—even wearable wrist—computers can now interface fully with larger portables and desktop machines, greatly increasing their usefulness without increasing their cost or size. At the other extreme, 386 processing power with 100 megabytes of hard-disk storage is now available in a laptop format, making it feasible for many of us to make our next desktop upgrade a portable—even to have a portable as our only computer in the future. This is becoming corporate policy in some organizations where productivity is most cost-effectively enhanced by issuing portables as both desktop replacements and work-to-go tools.

In Chapter 2, I outlined the basic categories of portables. Let us look now in more detail at these categories and consider their advantages and disadvantages.

Pocket Computers

Any computer that weighs less than one pound and measures no more than 4 × 9 × 1 inches can be considered pocketable. They are becoming increasingly powerful, so the better of them are ''true'' computers, but still with severe limitations.

Ask yourself seriously why you need a pocket computer—and you may well decide that you do not! They are attractive electronic gadgets that seem at first to be so useful, until you buy one and find it does not fit into your work-to-go lifestyle. Some owners find pocket computers so helpful that they become their most used device after a wristwatch. But for others they finish up in the back of a desk drawer, joining the collection of electronic marvels that did not deliver on their promises.

Indeed, if you want to store a limited number of contact names and addresses, maintain a summarized agenda that reminds you of appointments, and tell the time and date in different cities around the world, you can combine these functions in one compact, maximum-opportunity device. I can leave my desk and, with no effort at all, take with me an electronic database of all these personal time and information functions in my quartz computer *wristwatch*. It will hold eighty files of up to twenty-four characters each, is made by Seiko, and cost $30 from a mail order discounter, complete with the cable to interface with my PC. That's opportunity computing at an unbeatable price!

Macintosh enthusiasts have their equivalent—the Wristmac by Seiko—that will display a total of eighty screens in up to twelve files. It can be used as a stand-alone device to keep track of phone numbers, appointments, and notes, or in conjunction with a desktop or a Macintosh Portable. As this book went to press, this wrist system was retailing at around $250.

I've had a Casio watch that for years has kept a more limited contact database with unfailing reliability. It could hardly be more convenient to update; you just write letters and numbers on the watch face with your finger. No keyboard knowledge is required.

Somehow, in the rush to achieve business portability, people overlooked the digital watch as a minicomputer in its own right and it has acquired a down-market image. Maybe, if used in isolation, a wrist terminal cannot meet serious work-to-go needs, but it can serve well as a component of a fully functional system.

Pocket organizers offer far greater performance than digital wristwatches, but they have more limited use opportunity because you carry them rather than wear them. Casio, Psion, and Sharp are among the leading manufacturers of computers that fall well within the pocketable category. Typically, they can store about 3,000 telephone numbers or the equivalent of nearly 700 business cards in contact information, as well as the memo, time, scheduling, and other basic features a typical road warrior is likely to require.

Pocket organizers range from under $100 to over $300, with frequent deep discounting and a lot of confusion over what is included in the price for a particular offer. You can spend over $1,000 putting a pocket organizer system together, at which point you should pause and think whether a notebook computer does not make more sense. Peripherals such as a cable to transfer data to and from a PC, extra memory, applications functions modules, and the like can add substantially to the quoted price, yet they may be essential to give you a system with functions that meet your particular needs.

The Psion Organizer, for example, is incredibly versatile, but at the price of adding the appropriate datapaks to customize it. Put a system together and you can get a true pocket computer, but the price and inconvenience of plug-in accessories might be less attractive than going up to the next subcategory of pocketables, with their larger keyboards and screens.

Much the same applies to competing Sharp Wizard and Casio B.O.S.S. models. The Wizard has a great little screen and makes clever use of RAM/ROM plug-in cards for customizing and additional memory. If you are looking for a pocket system for a number of employees, Sharp has a corporate customizing service that might make all the difference in assembling and standardizing a portable system that really works for your organization.

The Casio B.O.S.S.—short for Business Organizer Scheduling System—is a particularly compact design with the advantage of a nearly conventional typewriter QWERTY keyboard. However, the keys on these pocket organizers are too small and too close together for serious and sustained inputting. You can overcome this if you input data through a larger computer.

The trend in this subcategory is to make pocket organizers function more efficiently in conjunction with desktops or large portables. Transferring data over wireless infrared links rather than cables and incorporating miniature modems for telephone data communications are examples of developments taking place. The options to transfer data from pocket organizers into the Macintosh environment are now increasing, so for many Mac users the pocket organizer with a data-transfer package may be the most cost-effective portability formula.

Inputting will become easier as better write-on screens offer viable alternatives to the miniscule keyboards. Pocket organizers must become easier to use in other respects, also. Complicated manuals put off potential users, something Sharp tried to overcome by issuing instructional videotapes.

However sophisticated the pocket organizers become, surveys of actual and potential users show that these computers are of limited value to many people, who find them too complex and without sufficient advantages over conventional appointment and address books or work planners. Traditional hard-copy media have the advantage of being able to create backup copies of critical data simply by making photocopies. But if you commit all your business-contact information to a pocket organizer and do not back it up by transferring the data to a computer, you are in deep trouble if the organizer is lost, stolen, or its batteries run down. And if you have to back up onto paper, then one of the main benefits of computerizing data is lost.

An alternative to the pocket organizer when work-to-go tasks are specialized is the new generation of high-power scientific pocket calculators that automate functions engineers and researchers need regularly. The best of these, such as the Hewlett-Packard range, can also interface with computers to transfer data.

The major limitation of pocket organizers will always be that manufacturers cannot shrink the keyboards and screens below a practical minimum. So for most business users who are able to accept more bulk and have larger pockets, there are better deals to be made by moving up in size to larger pocket computers. There are significant improvements in performance capabilities, noticeably in screen and keyboard usefulness and in overall versatility.

The choice in this sector includes the Laser PC3, packing nine useful applications built in, a reasonable keyboard, but a small display. The pricing is particularly attractive: well under $300. Although weighing around two pounds and costing over twice as much as the Laser, the Cambridge Z88 is worth a look because it has a number of unique features, including interfaces with both DOS and Mac systems, and a one-piece keyboard resisting dirt and moisture that could be a prime attraction for work under difficult conditions, but is not suitable for inputting substantial amounts of text.

The most notable pocket computer contenders at the time of writing are the Atari Portfolio listing at around $400 and the more expensive Poquet PC, at nearly $2,000. Both are true DOS computers weighing under a pound, with usable keyboards and screens.

With a little practice, a proficient typist—with small fingers!—can input at around thirty words per minute. Battery life is not a problem because they run on easily replaceable batteries that can last for up to 100 hours.

Although the Poquet is costly, it introduced what for some could be the priceless qualities of full DOS–compatibility in pocket format, with its 80C88 processor running at 7MHz, 512K RAM, DOS 3.3 on ROM, and a CGA-compatible display that is 80 columns by 25 lines. It is a great little computer built specifically for travel, with users reporting its survival through hazards ranging from spilled coffee to falls from taxis.

Neither the Portfolio nor the Poquet is as powerful as the latest generation laptops, but they are faster and more proficient at some tasks than the first desktop PCs, and that may well be all you need on the road. But do try out their keyboards and screens before committing yourself; some people hate them, others love them.

Notebook Computers

Placing a seven-pound weight limit and imposing letter-size dimensions on this portable computer category allows us to admit the smaller laptops to "notebook" membership. They also include superseded models now being discounted heavily because of small screens, limited memory, or other perceived disadvantages.

The Toshiba T1000 is the archetype and pioneer of the category, somewhat larger than a standard sheet of paper, but still small enough to fit into a briefcase or large hand or shoulder bag. The T1000 sets the basic price-performance-size parameters against which to judge the others. It weighs 6.4 pounds, has a single 720K disk drive, supertwist LCD, a full-function keyboard with 82 standard-spaced keys, and 512K of standard memory that can be expanded to 1.2MB. DOS is contained in ROM and Toshiba sells an add-in card that can be configured as a battery-backed RAM disk, as well as an internal modem and a comprehensive range of accessories.

The list price for the basic computer is about $1,000, but it is widely discounted at well under $700. There is a smaller, more powerful, more expensive T1000SE that beats the six pounds' weight barrier and uses an 80C86 CPU.

You may need to make few compromises on performance in the notebook category, particularly after the arrival of the Compaq LTE, which can be configured as a 286 system running OS/2. Although the NEC UltraLite and the Zenith MinisPort pioneered great performance in smaller packages than had been achieved before, they did so by sacrificing standard disk drives.

So again screens, keyboards, and storage media are the key items to check when comparison shopping in this sector. The GRiDPad is among the innovative designs that eliminate the keyboard entirely. It is truly an electronic notebook, one that you can hold in one hand while inputting by writing on the screen with a stylus.

Some notebook models do not compete equally with others in the range of ports they make available, and this could be crucial to particular applications involving peripherals such as a printer, mouse, or modem. Check particularly the convenience with which you can hook up an external keyboard and a monitor, should you want to extend the functionality of your portable.

Battery life and convenience also vary in this category. You can have the difference between four hours or more of use or just under two, depending on the type of battery and how well the system manages power consumption. The battery packs in this class are smaller than the categories that we examine later, so it makes sense to carry at least one spare battery if you anticipate computing for several hours away from an AC supply. The little Tandy 1100FD scores well on cost-efficiency, with an initial price under $1,000 and replacement battery packs available through Radio Shack for only $30.

Some of the notebooks make swapping batteries easy, while others are not so good in this respect. The most convenient are those that take standard disposable or rechargeable batteries. They vary greatly also in the speed of recharging and in the size of their electrical adapter-charger units. With some notebooks, what you gain in compactness and light weight can be offset by the clutter of peripherals necessary to make them useful.

Storage devices such as memory cards may be on the cutting edge of technology, reduce weight, and increase performance while conserving battery power, but they are much more expensive and far less versatile than the standard magnetic disks.

Screens and keyboards are subjective issues, but very critical for the individual user. Many of these notebook units save power and cost by not having backlit screens, but that can severely limit your computing opportunities.

To summarize, the trade-offs made to achieve light weight and size vary greatly with makes and models. Watch out for such marketing deceptions as weights quoted without the batteries—and in one case even the screen!—to qualify for the seven-pound weight limit.

Portability is the key attraction in this category, but look at the system in its entirety. The sleek little box that slips easily into your pocket or briefcase could be but the tip of the iceberg as far as bulk and weight are concerned. You may go for this category because you impose a weight limit of seven pounds, but you might finish by lugging around twice that much.

Mobile Computers

Arthur D. Little defines mobile computers as those able to run from their own batteries and that weigh under ten pounds. Here are three crucial pounds of difference between these computers and the notebook units. With mobile systems you reduce portability slightly, but the additional weight means you can move up to a clamshell design that is still reasonable carry-on baggage and with fewer compromises in screen and keyboard. Also, you can have at least 286 processing power, removable 3.5-inch disks and a large-capacity hard disk, internal modem and fax, plus an adequate selection of ports for peripherals.

Battery life is still a problem in this category, but many of the systems incorporate advanced power-management features, readily replaceable battery packs, or both. Remember to include the battery within the weight. A portable that is boosted to thirteen pounds or more when its battery is included becomes too heavy to carry around for long periods, especially if it is not the only item in your carry-on luggage.

Alternate Office Computers

By increasing the weight limit to under sixteen pounds, still able to run on battery power, but with high-quality displays to EGA or higher clarity, and with a hard disk mandatory, these portables can perform serious desktop tasks. In view of the many alternatives available to create

AC electricity from batteries (see Chapter 9), I suggest that we also include in this category portables that have all the Arthur D. Little qualifications except their own batteries.

This opens the door to powerful 386-level clamshells with large hard disks, and the lighter lunchbox style luggables that depend on AC power. It also admits systems that use their own lead-acid batteries. These have many advantages over nicads—the almost universal power source for laptops—but they are very heavy for their size.

For example, the Macintosh Portable may look lightweight, but it weighs in at around sixteen pounds with its batteries and hard disk. The Mac's weight penalty stems mainly from its lead-acid battery, which gives an outstanding eight or more hours of life and provides the power to make this a true alternative to a desktop system.

For much less weight—and less money—there are DOS systems that Mac users can adjust to fairly easily and which can exchange data with the Mac.

Also, there are alternatives to the genuine Apple, in the shape of portables using the Macintosh System from independent suppliers.

Desktop Substitutes

This category is defined essentially by performance: a central processing unit of at least 80286 level, an EGA or higher resolution display, and a hard disk. I have added the lunchbox portables weighing over sixteen pounds even if they have only basic PC, XT, or AT performance levels. They have the advantage of being comparatively easily expanded, as are their desktop relatives, to gain greater power or specific capabilities.

The desktop market grew so rapidly because so many independent manufacturers invaded it with different configurations of machines using the same standard components, selling at competitive prices. Many of the clones matured technologically to offer significantly better performance as well as more attractive pricing.

An area of portable computing suitable for a similar scenario is the lunchbox machine. Instead of being flat, and shaped and opening like a briefcase in the clamshell format, the lunchbox is squarer and upright—rather like a portable sewing machine. Typically, the keyboard detaches from the front upright side, revealing a pivoting LCD or gas plasma screen.

These computers are heavier—frequently well over twenty pounds—and bulkier, so they are far less convenient to carry around. However, because so many manufacturers compete in this area, buying in standard components to fit into very similar cases keeps down price and increases your options. You can customize and expand these machines economically. Theoretically, they should be easier to fix when things go wrong.

Quality, however, varies enormously among these units—the quality of both the hardware and the companies marketing them. Look particularly for clues of cost-cutting in such obvious features as the keyboard, the latches and fit on the casing, and the screen display.

Is the low price worth the risk that the new manufacturer or mail order house will not be around to support the product if things go wrong? On the other hand, because they need to inspire user confidence, the better mail order houses provide some of the most generous warranties. Just make sure you select a company with a reputation for delivering on its promises.

The value in this group of computers can be remarkable. For under $2,000 you can get a lunchbox configured with 386SX processor running at 16 MHz, a 40MB hard disk plus a high-density 3.5-inch floppy drive, 1MB of RAM, a large gas plasma display, and plenty of scope to expand its performance at reasonable cost. Some lunchboxes reduce their potential for increasing performance or adding features by having the expansion slots on the motherboard covered by the power unit, disk drives, or other components.

Many of the heavy, large, and high-performing alternate office computers depend on AC power—or have batteries that are soon exhausted. So standard desktop units may provide a more cost-effective mobile computer solution than having to pay a premium price and accept the design compromises inherent in portable systems. Portability and mobility do not necessarily mean frequent movement from place to place, but, perhaps, the ability to compute around the conventional office, factory, or warehouse. This is an important factor that might be just the key to finding your particular solution.

6

Interface Devices: Screens, Keyboards, Mice, and the Like

The most frustrating aspects of portable computers are their small screens and keyboards. These and other interfacing alternatives are the focus of this chapter.

A computer's display and keyboard are crucial because they are the elements of a system with which you have closest—and greatest—contact. However, if you find a combination of hardware features that approaches your ideal, but the system is handicapped by a poor screen or keyboard, you may well be able to overcome these defects. Using either software or hardware additions or modifications, it is possible to elevate a system to a configuration that offers you nearer to maximum computing opportunity.

Screens

Eye strain almost always emerges at the top of the list in surveys of what people working with computers believe to be their most serious hazard. It is ranked far higher than poor air quality or exposure to infectious diseases or hazardous materials such as asbestos. So it is not surprising that screen quality is the single greatest factor limiting the popularity of portable computers. Screens are getting better as the technology develops, but some are still pretty awful, especially for users aged over 35, when eyesight inevitably starts to decline.

Liquid Crystal Displays

Most portables have liquid crystal displays (LCDs). These have improved so rapidly that the best are very good, while portables with lower-quality displays can be picked up at bargain close-out prices. As an example, the early NEC Starlet is discounted from $999 to $179 and the Amstrad PPC 640 with a list price of $1,299 is priced at only $699 as I write this. (Deep discounts like these often refer to "remanufactured" equipment, which does not necessarily imply a computer that has been extensively used and then refurbished, but also covers demonstration units and those returned by customers after very little use—perhaps because they could not stand the small screens!)

All computer displays are made up of pixels—picture elements—playing the same role as the tiny dots in a screened photograph printed on paper. In newspapers the dots are large enough to be distinguished by the naked eye or under weak magnification. A display in only one color can be created by varying the light intensity of individual pixels, or the pixels may be controlled in clusters. A color display has pixels grouped in clusters containing at least one of each of the primary colors: red, green, and blue.

The liquid crystal displays function as their name implies. They are made up of rod-shaped crystal molecules that flow like a liquid. In their natural state, without any electrical current flowing through them, the crystals allow light to pass normally. When the computer is on and a pixel is activated by electrical impulses sent to the screen, the molecules move to change the direction of the light beams. By sandwiching the liquid crystals between polarizing filters and putting a reflector plate behind them, manufacturers get the crystals to reflect light to varying degrees as they are energized, so that you see images of different intensity against the screen's reflective backing.

The diagram shown in Figure 6-1 presents the principles. On the left are the molecules of a pixel that is not energized, and on the right those of a pixel with current flowing through it. This display, like all the better ones, twists the crystal molecules to accentuate the contrast.

LCDs are a very practical way to create a display for a laptop because the screen can be made flat, light, and robust, with low power consumption. The battery drain is far less to move the molecules than it would be actually to generate light to create a screen image.

However, relying on reflected light can be very limiting in the varying

Figure 6-1.   Twisted-Nematic liquid crystal display.

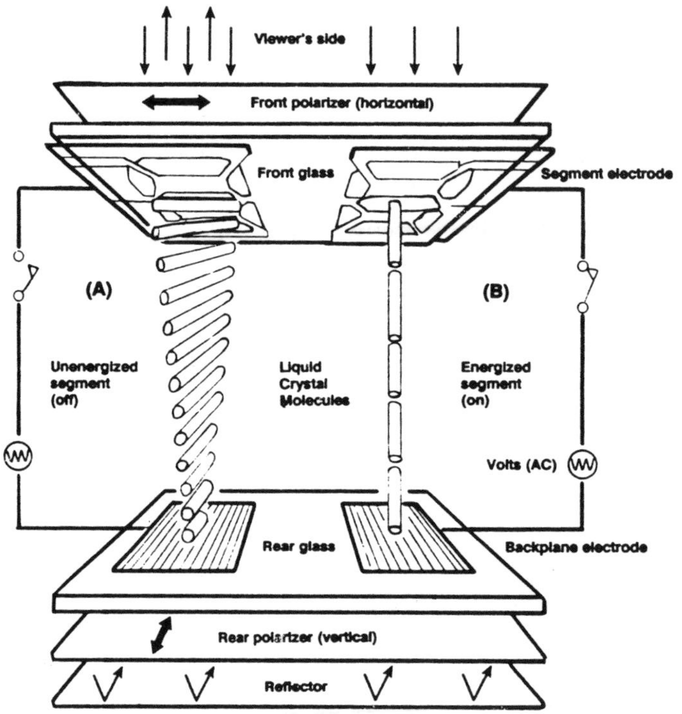

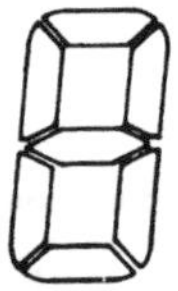

The two "figure-8" characters on the front glass of this example are made up of seven segments, allowing the digits 0 through 9 to be displayed.

conditions under which portable computers are used. You cannot twist them as easily to catch the light at the most favorable angle, as you can with a pocket calculator or wristwatch with an LCD display. If the ambient light is very high or low, then the screen may be impossible to read because too much or too little light is being reflected from it.

So most portable computers incorporate backlighting. They have a variable light source that shines through the reflective backing, increasing the contrast between the characters with their activated pixels and the background of the display. The penalty is that the backlight gobbles up electrical power. To conserve your batteries you need to switch the backlighting off, or keep it low, and work only with reflected light when it is adequate.

Once you buy a portable with an LCD that you do not like, you are probably stuck with it. Some manufacturers and third-party suppliers provide upgrade replacements that might add better supertwist LCDs or backlighting, but they can be disproportionately expensive.

LCDs are no longer automatically inferior to the cathode ray tube

(CRT) displays used in desktop monitors. Because they are flat and each pixel is controlled directly, LCDs do not have the bulk and distortion inherent in CRT displays.

There are new techniques using transistors to control each pixel, which give higher clarity as demonstrated in the Macintosh Portable. These thin film transistor LCDs, also called active-matrix LCDs, have made pocket color television sets possible and their use is being extended to the portable computer field.

So, in the years to come, LCDs will be commonplace for the computer monitors and television receivers in our offices and homes, as well as for the portables on the road. Price will come down with the anticipated high volumes and quality will steadily increase.

LCDs can produce good color displays, but they require strong backlighting, one of the main limiting factors in developing practical color displays for portable computers. However, most applications programs these days are designed to use color. Many portables incorporate color video electronics, even if their built-in displays are monochrome LCDs. This has the advantage of enabling portables to be hooked up to drive separate color CRT monitors, making the computer much more versatile.

There are problems when the colors of, say, your word processing software appear on the portable LCD screen in a limited range of gray tones. The boldface or underlining that stands out in contrasting colors when you see the program on a desktop monitor can almost disappear on the portable's monochrome LCD.

To overcome this, you need to experiment with the display options available with most applications programs until you get the settings that work best on a particular portable. This emphasizes again the need to customize your applications to run on your portable.

If you cannot get sufficient differentiation between the monochrome shades displayed when you run color applications text on your portable, there is a useful utility called MONO.COM contained in the March 28, 1989, edition of *PC Magazine*. You can download it from the PC MagNet on-line information service administered by CompuServe. This memory-resident utility program translates the color attributes that activate a color CRT display into different intensities of a single color, so that they stand out clearly on a portable's LCD—or any monochrome display, for that matter. It is not intended for use with graphics programs, only text.

If your portable has trouble displaying any applications programs, check with the technical support services of the manufacturer or software publisher, or with user groups, bulletin boards, shareware libraries, etc., for other solutions. One of the great things about computing is that if there is a problem, enterprising people look for solutions, which they are then ready to share.

In addition to running your portable with a compatible CRT monitor, there are other options available. For example, Toshiba offers a detachable EGA—Enhanced Graphics Adapter—LCD. It reflects a sharper and easier-to-read display in direct sunlight, and reduces battery consumption because there is no need for backlighting.

There is a good range, at increasingly attractive prices, of EGA CRT monitors that give better than standard CGA—Color Graphics Adapter—resolution. However, they are not compatible with most portables without the addition of a special EGA video display board that is difficult or impossible to fit into the typical portable.

Better still is the VGA—Video Graphics Array—display that is a hallmark of the PS/2 generation of personal computers. It requires special monitors and boards also, and it is not practical to upgrade most portables to take advantage of the superior VGA screen qualities.

EGA or VGA capabilities are coming to the high end of the portable computer market, as we will see when we look at the features of the more expensive systems shortly. I have seen color EGA CRT displays featured in ''assemble it yourself'' portables selling for as little as $1,250.

Gas Plasma Displays

Some portables have gas plasma screens, which are more expensive than LCDs, consume a lot of battery power, but can give a much more attractive display. They work by using electrodes to energize minute pockets of gas that form the pixels to create the display. The light—usually various shades of orange or red—consumes a lot of power, so most portables with gas plasma screens run off AC current. Those that have batteries may run down in less than half an hour, severely limiting their use away from an electrical outlet unless you have some of the mobile external power options described in Chapter 9.

Gas plasma displays tend to be much crisper and easier on the eyes than LCDs or many CRT displays, and they function well under virtually all lighting conditions and angles of view. A sales demonstration on a portable with a gas plasma screen can be far more attractive and viewable by more people at the same time than one on an LCD.

The service life of gas plasma displays generally has been far less than for LCDs or CRTs, and they have only recently acquired the capacity to generate scales of contrast, the equivalent of the gray scales on other monochrome screens or the colors on a CGA, EGA, or VGA monitor. So approach a portable with a gas plasma screen with caution; you may grow to love it or hate it.

An interesting gas plasma development was Toshiba's introduction of the first battery-powered portables able to drive a monochrome gas plasma display and a color monitor or projector at the same time. The obvious application for this is presentation graphics.

Electroluminescent Displays

These portable displays work by passing an electric current through a phosphorescent material such as a zinc and manganese compound. The pixels glow brightly and the display can be seen easily under the most adverse conditions. That is why EL displays are favored by the military. They have become a lot cheaper to produce in recent years, and power consumption has improved to place EL displays between LCDs and gas plasma in battery demand.

Although not readily available yet in commercial systems, EL displays could evolve to play an important part in the future of portable computing.

Other Viewing Devices

Presentation Displays

You can project very large displays easily and economically from most portable computers by hooking up a panel to go onto an overhead projector, as you would a transparency. This is one of the easiest ways to make a presentation.

These LCD panels have evolved to give good results in either monochrome or color, and they can eliminate the need to create either 35mm slides or overhead transparencies from your computer-generated graphics. You can create and show your presentation entirely with your portable, making it more attractive, reliable, and a lot easier to move from place to place. You can also modify the presentation while on the road.

Similar results can be achieved by using software programs and hardware adapters and connections to send your portable's output to a video projector.

Virtual Screen Displays

Becoming readily available for the first time in 1990 was a new generation of computer displays that could be significant in the future. For virtual screen displays, the size of the screen is not a limitation because you look through it to see an image that can be almost any size. A one-inch window opens into a display that can be fifty or more times larger—as big as any desktop monitor.

Devices such as Reflection Technology's Private Eye can have many applications. A worker assembling components or servicing equipment can call up diagrams or specifications from a computer database and refer to them superimposed over the work piece (see Figure 6-2). A doctor dealing with either routine or emergency situations can access a patient's records or medical references. Linking the virtual display to a telephone opens up a host of other possibilities (see Figure 6-3). Combining the virtual display

Figure 6-2.   Headset.

with portable computing and cellular telephone and paging technology can link visuals with voice or text messages and with data in many practical ways.

This is coming close to the ultimate in opportunity computing as far as screen display is concerned. The technology has been described as virtually putting your brain on-line, because the image is superimposed on the task or situation while your hands and eyes are free to carry out other functions. Now full-size screens become feasible for even very small pocketable computers previously forced to use tiny LCDs that are unable to cope with graphics or significant amounts of text.

In a virtual display, a full 720×280 pixel screen appears to float at normal reading distance in front of the eye. Higher-resolution displays are possible, and the technology is very flexible in terms of colors and other features. The apparent projected image is created by an array of very small light-emitting diodes (LEDs), a scanning mirror, and advanced optics and microelectronics. The power consumption is very small.

As this book went to press, the Private Eye was being incorporated into a whole range of innovative portable information products as well as

Figure 6-3.   "Eye" phone.

being packaged for sale directly to end users to apply to existing portable computers. The products include a pocket paperless fax machine, various portable personal computers and electronic reference books, and medical applications.

This unique display is making possible miniature full-function portable workstations for maintenance technicians, engineers, doctors, military personnel, and other computer users whose opportunities for work outside the office have been limited by display screen size and clarity.

As with all displays, the Private Eye may not be ideal for your needs. Some who have tried it have experienced difficulty adjusting to this most unusual way of looking at an image, while others have reported headaches. But the advantages are so enormous that for many portable computer users it will prove indispensable.

Some Low-Tech Display Options

Fresnel Screen

Advanced technology may be great but a low-tech solution might be the immediate answer for you. I transformed a small hard-to-read laptop screen by mounting a plastic Fresnel magnifier in front of it. You can get these from stationery and drug stores for a few dollars; they are light, flat, and strong.

You need to space the Fresnel screen the desired distance from the display. The easiest way of doing this is to experiment with plastic foam strips, finding the preferred thickness and then glueing the foam on the perimeter of the magnifier. It may rest well against the screen of a typical clamshell laptop, or you may need to fix it in place with self-adhesive Velcro tabs.

A high-quality Fresnel screen is available for the E-Z View computer monitor hood and periscope. It can substantially increase the apparent size of image of a laptop or desktop display. Although the hood itself was designed for a conventional desktop monitor, it can be adapted for use with some portables.

Developed by a leading eye surgeon, the hood's periscope arrangement of mirrors enables the display to be positioned right in front of the keyboard.

There is less eye strain because glare is reduced, and the mirrors intensify the contrast of the image as well as enable it to be increased in size by adding either a magnifying mirror or an enlarging Fresnel screen, depending on the degree of magnification required.

Shades

An even lower-tech solution to glare on a screen is to make a shade from cardboard that fastens over the screen with tape or Velcro tabs. A range of shades is available ready-made from Compu-Shade (916/933-2228, or 800/527-5048 outside California).

Keyboards

Keyboards come close to screens in the frustrations they cause portable computer users. They are the only part of the system with which you have continual direct physical contact, often for hours or days—years on end if you use a computer to earn your living. On an average writing day, I hit the keys over fifty thousand times. A mediocre keyboard is worse for me than a pair of ill-fitting shoes. I get pain in my fingers that extends up my arms; my stress level builds in direct proportion to the degree of frustration being generated by a keyboard that is badly designed or built.

Some portable keyboards are truly awful. They may be very difficult to use from the day you buy them, or they can fail quickly because they cannot sustain even moderately intense use. One well-known model has a tendency to eject its spring-loaded key caps—shooting them out like little missiles—which adds a new dimension to personal computing, but greatly inhibits productivity!

Even if you are not a proficient typist, give the portable's keyboard a thorough test drive before you buy. Find out its quirks—for example, squishy, undersized keys with an indefinite movement or that are too close together to use comfortably.

Do you want a positive movement with a definite click that helps your rhythm? Some typists need audible feedback and find it difficult to adjust to a soft, silent board. You can get this sound with software programs if you find it essential, although if you are switching from a typewriter to a computer keyboard for the first time, allow a few days to adjust. You may well prefer a silent, smooth action after you have become used to it. People who need to take notes in meetings or use their portables in libraries, courtrooms, or lecture halls require silent keyboards.

Some larger portables have full-size keyboards with a layout identical to desktop systems that follow IBM's standard and extended models. More compact laptops with keyboards that are typically a third smaller than standard have the keys placed closer together, and incorporate some quirky layouts and key combinations that may greatly hinder your work flow.

Pay particular attention to the location of keys you use frequently. Most laptops and smaller portables eliminate the separate numeric keypad. This can be a disadvantage if you input a lot of numbers. A popular alternative is to "embed" the numeric keypad into the keyboard, so that the numbers share keys with functions or characters. Some such layouts are infuriating, especially if you are working on spreadsheets or statistical reports and have to keep switching back and forth to activate and deactivate the numeric keys.

Check particularly for the cursor control keys, which may be shared with the PAGE UP and PAGE DOWN, HOME, and END functions. This can be particularly frustrating for word processing and database users. Awkward placement of the cursors is a handicap for everyone, especially as portables tend to be used less with mice than desktops.

Frequently, portables adopt the inverted T layout, with the LEFT and RIGHT arrows flanking the DOWN arrow at the bottom, and the UP arrow central and above, forming the leg of the T. Most people adjust to this fairly easily, and it is better than having the cursor keys laid out in a line or an L shape, or when they share a function with other keys or there is an awkward hand movement to activate the cursor and a control or function key at the same time.

Some keyboards have full-size keys crammed together. This increases the chances of miskeying and wastes time making corrections. It can be a big help if the keys you use most are distinctive and larger than normal, particularly the ENTER, SHIFT, ALT, BACKSPACE, CONTROL, and DELETE keys. The location of the delete key can be particularly important if you have become accustomed to using the DELETE and INSERT keys frequently as a fast way of moving blocks of text.

Keyboard Adjustments

If you do a lot of number work or the cursor arrangement on your portable's keyboard does not prove adequate, there are a number of numeric pads supplied as accessories, some also incorporating better cursor and function key layouts. But these add-ons can weigh almost a pound and take up room, and you may not have a slot available to accommodate one. An auxiliary numeric keyboard sold by Traveling Software features the keys necessary for spreadsheet applications, symbols, functions, and cursor control. It shares the parallel printer port with the printer's plug, so both devices can work at the same time. If you do a great deal of inputting, consider plugging a full-size keyboard into your portable.

Manufacturers who try to save space on portable keyboards by reducing the length of the space bar make lots of enemies, as do those who opt for moving the CAPS LOCK key to where the CONTROL key is normally located. There is a fix for such situations in some utility programs available as shareware. In fact, you can use software to fine-tune a portable keyboard to your preferences, altering whatever the keys do. Some word processing software also gives you great flexibility in this respect.

Many applications programs these days have facilities for macros, linking a whole string of frequently executed keystroke sequences so that they are completed by hitting just one or two keys. There are also utility programs specially for this purpose and self-adhesive labels to put on the keys to remind you what they do.

Creative use of macros can reduce your keystrokes in a working day by 25 percent or more, which adds up to thousands of physical actions. This can make a big difference when coping with a less-than-ideal keyboard. Effective use of a mouse can further reduce keyboard activity, as we will examine shortly.

A change of applications programs (or perhaps studying for the first time the manual for the one you have) can save thousands of keystrokes by making better use of fast key actions. For example, I can print this chapter of the book by making over twenty keystrokes in Microsoft Word to format and sending the text to my printer—or I can do it in a flash by pressing CONTROL and F8 at the same time.

If you are new to keyboarding, you might like to start off with an option that is not viable for those of us accustomed to the standard keyboard. (The QWERTY configuration is a legacy from the early mechanical typewriters to slow down fast typists so they did not jam the mechanism. You cannot jam computer keyboards however fast you go because they have buffers and circuitry to make each action take its place in an electronic queue from your fingers to the screen, even if you hit several keys at the same time.) The Dvorak keyboard has a layout that is inherently more efficient, putting the most used keys in the places where they can be reached easily. Dvorak keyboards are available from a number of mail order houses and retail stores. Software can reassign the keys on your portable to the Dvorak layout, or you can plug in a separate Dvorak keyboard.

Touch typists might rely more than they realize on the small raised bumps of the home keys that provide tactile keyboard reference points. You may not properly appreciate them until they are no longer there. Your portable almost certainly does not have these bumps on the F and J keys, but you can add them with a small and carefully applied drop of sealing or candle wax.

Comfort Adjustments

If you are used to working with the keyboard tilted toward you and find with a new portable that your hands and wrists get tired more quickly, this could be because the angle of the keys is not comfortable. The remedy is obvious: prop the back of the portable up and change the angle of the screen if the two are integrated. If the keyboard can be separated, then it probably has two foldout feet at the back, so that the angle can be adjusted.

A common cause of discomfort—even pain—when switching to a portable is not the fault of the equipment but reflects the changes in the way you use it. The discomfort is often a direct consequence of computing in places not designed for working at screens and keyboards. For example, your office desk and chair may be ergonomically correct for computing, but the kitchen chair and table where you use your portable may be higher or lower than normal. This can generate all kinds of aches and pains.

If your fingers have to reach higher than your elbows to hit the keys, this can cause considerable strain. The ideal is to have your fingers slightly lower and with no sharp angles at the wrist or finger joints. It really does make a difference when you get as close as possible to the ideal relationship between machine and body.

Now that portables are being used extensively in cars and trucks, there is a need to carry and mount them securely. One solution, the Mead-Hatcher Auto-Pro Workstation, is available from Traveling Software and other vendors for about $100 (see Figure 6-4). Obviously, computing while driving is not to be recommended, but this device positions the laptop conveniently for use when parked, and can display street maps and route guides to the driver while en route.

Keyboard Maintenance

I keep my desktop keyboard going year after year by taking it apart every so often and giving it a thorough cleaning. It is amazing what dust and debris can accumulate to inhibit efficiency. Beneath each key cap is a small switch that activates the circuitry in which a microprocessor turns your manual instructions into electronic pulses and code. Even just a tiny foreign object in the mechanism can make a key misbehave.

The keyboard, being one of the few mechanical components of a

Figure 6-4.   The Mead-Hatcher Auto-Pro Workstation.

computer, is among the most likely to fail. The biggest problem is dirt or moisture dropping through the spaces between the keys—a problem aggravated by personal habits such as smoking and eating or drinking while working.

Unfortunately, you cannot take the typical portable's keyboard apart to clean it. Everything underneath is jammed in so tightly that you can easily damage a component or loosen a connection—and you might not be able to get it all back together again, either. So keeping a portable's keyboard clean is important. I use a combination of a soft cosmetic brush and a can of compressed air, being careful that dust is lifted up and away, not forced down beneath the keys. If you work or travel under particularly dusty conditions, it is worth having a photographic blower brush for this simple preventive maintenance. These soft brushes attached to a plastic air pump cost and weigh very little, and every photographic supply department stocks them.

If your portable is used under particularly adverse conditions, put a flexible cover over the keyboard. These are customized for different models and cost about $25 from mail order and retail stores. Made of a special flexible plastic, the cover fits snugly over the keyboard and yet you can continue to use the keys almost normally.

Anything stuck to the keys or the portable's casing—like marmalade from the breakfast you had in your hotel room while working at your computer—should be cleaned off with a lightly moistened swab, ensuring that not even a drop of liquid can fall or be squeezed into the electrical circuits.

The safest solvent is distilled or clean tap water with a trace of soap. Because the composition of plastics varies so much, any cleaning solvent can pose hazards, although a careful test of the head cleaner sold for tape recorders should show this to be effective without being damaging.

Grain alcohol can be a potent solvent, and in an emergency I've removed stains when traveling by moistening a Q-Tip in a glass of vodka. But this is not recommended, because most booze contains oils, flavorings, and other substances that may not react well with the plastic of your portable's keys or casing. There is a technical grade of isopropyl alcohol that professionals use for various cleaning purposes, including cleaning the rollers inside a mouse, which tend to pick up dirt easily.

Other Keyboard Options

Consider an often overlooked form of keyboard that might be a good match for you. Wireless keyboards are compact, portable units that are particularly useful in making presentations without being tethered to a computer. There are several models on the market; some work through the serial port so they can be used with portables that do not have a keyboard port.

Another option to put more mobility into a system is a device called Station Doubler, from Support Systems International. This enables two keyboards and monitors to share one computer from distances over 500 feet away. It could, for example, be the solution for controlling inventory in a warehouse, or to achieve remote control in some school and office situations.

Mice

After keyboards, the most common interface is a mouse. Mice are an integral part of Macintosh philosophy and they are gaining ground in the DOS world. Even if you have not felt the need for a mouse in your desktop system, keep an open mind about one for your portable. A mouse is a more convenient, faster, and less stressful way of issuing instructions than an inadequate keyboard.

Few portables come equipped with a mouse, and it is often a problem finding a place for it during a trip, as well as devising a level surface on which it can function. Using a mouse in an aircraft can be especially difficult.

The Macintosh Portable has turned the mouse upside down and converted it into a built-in tracking ball. A PC compatible, the Altima, has a special compartment to accommodate its optomechanical mouse. Even if Altima has a somewhat quirky layout for its cursor keys, the detachable 101 keyboard with numeric keypad, integral modem, paper-white screen, and mouse in a house are great portable computing features. Judges in the U.S. Court of Appeals use these mouse-driven laptops on the road.

Mice contain a rolling ball linked to a simple mechanism that rotates two slotted disks at right angles to each other. Light-emitting diodes shine through the slots, generating electrical signals relayed to the computer. As the mouse moves, the slotted disks rotate, the signals vary, and the computer gets continually updated information on the coordinates of the mouse's location.

It's rather like satellite navigation for oil tankers, but on a much smaller scale. The position of the mouse is translated into the position of the cursor on the display screen, and then actions are executed at those cursor locations by pressing buttons on top of the mouse housing. This point-and-click procedure is a natural and efficient interface, with many advantages over the keyboard.

Types of Mice

Mice come in two species: bus and serial. They look and behave the same, but have substantial differences, especially for portable computer users. The serial mouse hooks up to the serial port, so you need a spare one or face the prospect of connecting and disconnecting the mouse every time you want to use the printer or some other peripheral sharing the same port.

The bus mouse comes with its own card that plugs into one of the empty expansion slots available in most desktop personal computers, but not in many portables. Even some of the lunchbox portables don't have the slots available that may be listed in their specifications. (The slots may be there, but you can't use them because they are obscured by power packs or other components.) Fortunately, some bus mice come with compact cards that might fit some portables.

Most applications programs will run with either bus or serial mice, but that is not always the case and you should check for compatability before buying. Some programs—CAD software, for example—are so heavily dependent on mouse input that they take over much of the control from the mouse's own software driver, and can pose compatibility problems.

Finding somewhere for your mouse to move smoothly can be difficult on the road. There is, for example, no drop-down table in a commercial jet that provides enough comfortable space for both a laptop and a mouse. That's why a stationary mouse can be the best solution. The concept is incorporated into the Macintosh Portable and will be appearing more in DOS systems. It can be purchased as an accessory for between $70 and $150.

Stationary mice are various configurations of what are basically mice turned on their backs. Instead of moving a mouse around, you roll the ball in different directions to change the position of the cursor. While stationary mice may look much the same, there are substantial differences in their ergonomic efficiency and how the ball is moved and the buttons are pressed. Some encourage a natural thumb and finger movement; others can be very awkward. Take a test drive before purchasing.

Mice are also getting more sophisticated, increasing their use with portables of all kinds. For example, the Super Mouse from International Computer Software can be tuned so it will function better in a small space. You need to move it only an inch or two to position the cursor anywhere on the screen.

Mouse Maintenance

Traveling mice tend to get dirty far quicker than those who lead a sedentary desktop life. The principles for cleaning most makes and models are similar.

After disconnecting the lead at the computer, turn the mouse onto its back and unscrew the retaining plate that holds the ball in place. (Some models have screws holding the plate in place.) Turn the mouse over again and the ball should fall safely into your palm; if not, gently shake to dislodge it. Rub the ball with a soft, clean cloth or dab at the surface with sticky tape to pick up dust and lint, being careful not to leave any of the tape's adhesive behind.

In most cases, you will need only to clean inside the socket to remove any dust, hairs, or lint that may have accumulated. Use one of the miniature battery-powered vacuum cleaners sold in drug stores and computer outlets or a swab slightly moistened with alcohol or tape head cleaner.

If problems persist, or there is a substantial buildup of dirt and debris, you may need to unscrew the bottom of the mouse housing. Don't poke around inside with anything hard and sharp, and keep the mouse inverted over a tray or tabletop so you will not lose any small component that might fall out.

Advances in Mouse Technology

The Swiss Army Knife equivalent in computer mice is the Power-Mouse (Figure 6-5). When I asked ProHance Technologies, Inc., president Kirk MacKenzie what benefits portable users can expect from his device, he had no hesitation in predicting productivity increases for the average laptop user by a factor of 3 or 4. Users report an easily achieved doubling of speed when working with spreadsheets. At under $300, it is a unique approach to enhancing inadequate portable keyboards and bringing the advantages of a mouse to any software.

PowerMouse adds forty buttons to the conventional mouse, which has only two or three. All forty buttons can be programmed to do long and complex sequences of instructions that normally require a great deal of keyboarding. So, in one very portable device you get the mouse, a numeric keypad, a function keypad, remote control of your computer, and 250 programmable commands—all within easy reach of the fingers on one hand.

By defining the buttons for the program you are using, you can replace any keyboard key or any sequence of keystrokes. The accompanying software customizes the PowerMouse for a wide range of applications programs, or you can do it yourself for your favorite applications and method of working. The great advantage is that you can bring mouse power to software not written to support mouse input, increasing your productivity in familiar programs.

First-time computer users, or those not comfortable with keyboarding, should look at this option carefully, because knowing that many of the limitations of the keyboard can be overcome could influence your choice of portable computer. The PowerMouse also has obvious applications for the handicapped, and for users concerned about carpal tunnel and other repetitive stress health problems stemming from intensive keyboard operation.

Other Input Devices

Keyboards and mice are far from being the only ways to control a portable computer. *Bar code technology* is increasingly a way of

Figure 6-5. The PowerMouse.

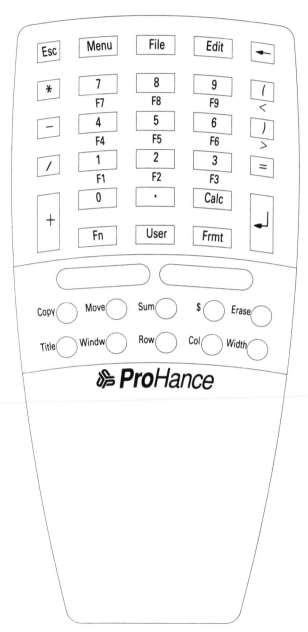

inputting or accessing data and can be integrated with most laptops very easily while leaving the keyboard functional, so that input by keystrokes and an intelligent bar code reader wand can be mixed.

When a lot of text needs to be inputted and hard copies already exist, consider reducing the keyboarding by reading the hard copy with a *scanner* and optical character recognition software. Most scanners, however, require add-in cards, and there is difficulty fitting these into most portables. That could be another reason for adding an external expansion unit to your laptop, or for considering a versatile lunchbox machine with more space in which to grow internally.

Various *touch-screen* notebook and laptop models are coming onto the market, some combining elements of portable technology to greatly extend their usefulness. The DynaBook touch screen recognizes some 40,000 touchable points and sixteen levels of pressure. You can use this portable for many applications without needing a keyboard at all. If you want to use a conventional keyboard, you call one up on the touch screen.

Another attraction of the DynaBook was that the screen was detachable— a feature that should be standard on most portables. That increases your computing opportunities enormously. For example, if you are working under a car or fixing a complex piece of industrial machinery, you can position the DynaBook's screen so that you can see it comfortably, and then display any diagrams or references you need from the complete workshop manual run from the built-in CD-ROM diskdrive, which is capable of holding 300,000 printed pages. Some pioneers in this field ran into problems, before the touch-screen and CD-ROM markets became commercially viable.

Another leader in touch-screen technology is GRiD Systems Corporation. Their portable GRiDPad recognizes printed *handwriting*, operates for up to eight hours on its internal battery, and converts readily to a conventional computer. This notepad type of portable is the electronic equivalent of a clipboard, particularly useful when working standing up, for filling in forms, and for employees who are not proficient with either a keyboard or conventional computer usage. It has been hailed as the first blue collar computer, but the price is still near the executive level.

Good portables are designed to cope with the rigors of life on the road. The GRiD laptop used by Bill Hazen, television announcer for the Indiana Pacers National Basketball Association team, has survived several falls caused by both balls and players (see Figure 6-6). Bill uses his computer to keep track of player statistics.

Sony's entry into the field of portable computers that efficiently accept *handwritten input* is giving further impetus to one of the major growth areas for portable computing. Japan has the edge over the United States in developing applications for fuzzy logic technology, which moves

Figure 6-6.   Bill Hazen, television announcer for the NBA Indiana Pacers, and his GRiD laptop at courtside.

computers from the era in which they learned to respond with increasing speed to basic yes or no situations, to being able to process more ambiguous information such as the quirks of handwriting or speech.

Automatic speech recognition (ASR) is developing so rapidly that its delayed application to portable computing is more as a result of management attitudes and ignorance than technical limitations. Most professions or specialities need equipment with no more than a 10,000-word vocabulary to generate reports or record information. There are several ASR systems that can be trained to recognize such a vocabulary and so digitize dictation.

Basic voice-recognition systems that do not need the hardware or software power to cope with extended vocabularies can be great productivity enhancers for portable computing situations. For about $150 you can get the hardware that fits into an eight-bit expansion slot, a microphone, and the accompanying software requiring 256K of memory to reduce long sequences of keyboard instructions to single-word commands.

For example, the Voice Master Key recognizes 64 words and phrases and stores up to 256 macros. That may not sound like a lot of capacity, but it can be more than enough for many situations. A police patrol that has stopped a suspect can run a license check on the car with a spoken request while still monitoring the behavior of the suspect. The officer stands by his patrol car and speaks through the window. The first single-word command activates the portable computer to make a radio connection with the dispatcher, then the officer reads out the license plate number, which the computer digitizes and transmits.

The voice-recognition system works with most existing business software. Separate sound files can be created by the user to meet individual needs, so you might have one set of voice instructions for your word processing, another for your database, a third for your spreadsheet.

Voice recognition is an example of what is perceived to be futuristic technology but that is available now and can be used on portable equipment at reasonable cost. We do not have long to wait before it will become routine for managers on the road to dictate their electronic mail and other correspondence into ASR programs running on portable computers. This application can be ideal in demanding travel situations when a keyboard, mouse, or other input device cannot be used. It represents one of the most exciting areas for rapid expansion of portable computing. For example, doctors moving rapidly around a hospital emergency room will both speak the record of what they are doing and get voice prompts to guide them through diagnostic procedures. A technician with no keyboard skills at all—and wanting to keep his hands free anyway—can use basic words or phrases to call up displays of the relevant pages of a whole library of repair manuals. Such opportunities are possible from portable computers and peripherals that we can wear. The Voice Master Key comes complete with headset and microphone at a cost less than that for many portable modems or power packs.

It is also possible to wear a computer input device that provides a remarkable direct physical link between human and machine. The $8,000 DataGlove senses finger movements and transmits them to the computer. For a hundredth of the price, you can sample the technology in Mattel's Power Glove for Nintendo video games.

The next development in this field is DataSuit, a full-body sensor that makes the wearer part of the on-screen computer action in animation sequences. This device has great potential for helping develop robots that more accurately mimic human movements. Its potential is expanded if it can be taken out of the laboratory and used in field situations in conjunction with powerful portables.

Another exciting area in which technology is eliminating the keyboard is music. Already there are software and portable computers designed specifically to create music, so you can carry around with you the equivalent of a full symphony orchestra. Now researchers are enabling music to be created in portable equipment just by moving the hands in light beams. Eventually that could lead to a completely different way for humans to communicate with computers, making keyboards and mice obsolete as the input devices in many work-to-go situations.

7

Power, Performance, and Storage Options

Remember the days when autos were marketed with emphasis on horsepower? We have grown out of that phase, having learned the hard way that impressive advertising figures did not necessarily translate to either travel speed or efficiency.

It will take longer for the majority of computer users to understand their technology sufficiently to grasp the meaning—and too often the deception—behind the storage capacity figures used to convey a power image for portables.

For example, the size of a storage medium can sound very impressive, but the time it takes to find a specific file can be far more important. A CD-ROM disk can give even a modest portable direct access to over 300,000 pages of data, but the benefits are limited if it takes ten times longer to find the data you need than from an ordinary hard disk or floppy. The comparison becomes even more odious if the information is neither very valuable nor very topical, as is the case with much data that so far has been committed to CD-ROM.

Also, you can spend $1,000 more to get theoretically greater memory and performance from an integral or external hard disk, but finish up with a slower system than if you had organized your computing to make best use of much less capacity. If you are thinking of upgrading because your existing system has become too slow, your best option might well be to spend $3 on a shareware hard disk management utility rather than hundreds of dollars to move from 20MB to 40MB.

You should look carefully at the various ways of storing data and programming, and learn how they are defined in terms of capacity and performance, before determining the most appropriate for your computing needs. In particular, do not be persuaded by peer pressure to get more than you need. As I write this book on an 8088 heavily discounted, obsolete Zenith laptop without a hard drive, the latest issue of *PC Magazine* is open beside me. It contains such statements as:

No serious portable should be without a hard disk.

Don't settle for anything less than a 386SX machine if this is to be your only machine.

Portables are the only format in which buying a 80286-based machine still makes sense.

Also:

The 8086-based personal computer is a dying class.

Such arrogant nonsense does a disservice to the development of portable computing. The implication that you *must* have high power and performance inhibits the growth of computing opportunity and wastes both personal and corporate resources in a cycle of rapid obsolescence. Affordability and ease of use are more important for most applications.

Japanese industry tends not to be so easily seduced into the technology race and instead puts more effort and investment into human factors such as training. It is obviously paying off.

Surveys in both Europe and the United States show that an overwhelming majority of CEOs doubt their businesses get satisfactory returns from investments in information technology (IT). There is growing resistance to linking corporate profitability with yet another new generation of increased IT power, when the hardware and software that companies already have is not being used cost-effectively.

Nevertheless, many executives are now using laptops and are able to make informed decisions about what this particular category of computers can do for their business. They are better able to relate IT power to the bottom line. Senior managers are less likely to be impressed by immaculate desktop-published requisition requests in five different fonts, seeking to justify 386 laptops costing over $5,000 when the department is already not making full use of its Toshiba 1000s costing under $700.

I interviewed many portable users to establish how the hardware and software are applied on the road. Almost without exception, the most creative applications of portable computing to increase productivity are with systems at the lower end of the price scale, well away from the cutting edge of the technology. A particular example is the pioneering applications of databases by users of askSam, a program that has been around since 1985 and runs happily on any laptop with just 256K, a single floppy drive, and PC or MS-DOS of 2.0.

Mobile Office, which, unlike many magazines, tries not to get carried away by the electronics industry's plethora of new product releases, ran a series of profiles on work mobility. One of the stars was successful publisher Wayne Green, who can obviously afford the latest and most powerful, but sees no reason to change the Radio Shack 100 portable that has served him well for six years.

With the exception of the power users (generally the computer professionals), it is not the speed and memory of a portable that dictates how beneficial it is to your work. How effective you are in making best use of the hardware and software you have got is more important. Ansell Adams is an object lesson. The marketing hype for continually higher technology films, lenses, and cameras conflicts with the hard reality: the most praised and still most impressive photographs of the United States were taken by Adams, using materials and equipment now many generations back in theoretical obsolescence. The creativity and quality of the human beings using the machines is what really counts—a thought that should remain with us as we review how portable computing power is measured.

Memory

Computers are basically very efficient machines at switching electrical current on and off. They process data in an extremely rapid sequence of on and off switching. These pulses of electricity are controlled by the code written into the software programming, and also by the conversion of the data into a digitized form of on and off instructions.

What makes the computer so versatile is its ability to save and recall those instructions to and from memory storage. Memory is the most important performance factor to consider for your portable. In theory, the more memory you have the better—as long as you make good use of it and it does not require excessive trade-offs in cost and portability.

There are four main types of memory store for portables: magnetic disks (floppy and hard), random access memory (RAM), read only memory (ROM), and optical read only memory on compact disks (CD-ROM). In each case, programming codes or data are converted into a form that the memory can both retain and release back to you when you need it.

Magnetic Disks

Floppy Disks. By far the most common form of memory storage for personal computers is magnetic disks—both removable and those that are an integral part of the machine. Removable disks give your data far greater mobility, extending far beyond your system, but only if the disks can be read easily elsewhere.

These words were written on my houseboat in San Francisco Bay. Along with thousands of others they went onto a small disk, slipped into a Federal Express envelope, and traveled over 2,000 miles to New York for processing into this book.

My work grows wings and flies around the world because it is stored in the memory of standard disks that all my publishers use. Those aspects of portability and transferrability are very important when considering memory and data storage. Newer and ever-cleverer ways of committing computerized data to magnetic memory are emerging all the time, especially with marketing pressures to make portables smaller and more powerful. But oddball ways of storing data, however technologically brilliant, are of little value to the typical user if they eliminate opportunities for efficiency, productivity, convenience, and economy because they are not compatible with the systems with which you need to exchange data.

The signals for electrical activity that the computer can understand are stored on disks in the form of magnetic code—minute magnets created by the disk drive's read-write head. The disks have a metallic oxide coating similar to that on audio- or videocassette tapes. As the disk spins, the electric code signals from the computer are transmitted to this coating by the read-write head's electromagnets positioned just above the surface. The head aligns the miniature magnets in the oxide coating in different directions, depending on whether the instruction is for an on or an off switching action. When the stored memory is required again, the read part of the head retrieves those instructions and the computer converts them from magnetic form back into electrical pulses.

When you buy blank disks, they are usually supplied without any magnetic orientation or information on them—just the magnetic coating. The computer must format them to provide the structure necessary to receive the information that will be stored in memory. It's a process rather like creating file folders with reference tabs for a filing cabinet. During the formatting, the read-write head divides the magnetic coating on each side of the disk into a series of tracks—like the drawers of a filing cabinet—with each track further divided into sectors—like the divisions in each drawer into which file folders can be placed.

When the disk has been formatted, the read-write head can be directed to tracks and sectors to store data or programming codes and, just as important, find its way back to the same place when you need to recall that information from memory. Most disk problems that prevent you from recovering data—be they from mechanical failure, software bugs, or computer viruses—are because the head cannot find the data on the disk. The data may not be destroyed, simply missing.

Unlike the filing cabinet analogy, computerized data are stored on each disk in a fragmented manner, so that the contents of one file folder can be scattered around in various sectors and tracks on the disk's surface, wherever there are empty spaces. The File Allocation Tables (FAT) function in the operating system software keeps track of where the fragments of data are stored. If the FAT does not function properly, the computer cannot go into the memory store and reconstruct the file when you want to recall the data. That is why several computer viruses are targeted at the FAT. If you cannot find an important file, it may still be recoverable if you use a powerful disk management utility or get a human expert to persuade the FAT to cooperate.

Most portables use 3.5-inch disks contained in plastic cases. They are popularly known as microfloppies despite their hard plastic shells, because they are miniature versions of the flexible 5.25-inch floppy disks that are standard for desktop systems. Despite their smaller size, microdisks are so efficient that they can store more data than their bigger predecessors, are more robust, and are rapidly becoming the standard for desktops also. However, with most of the 30 million personal computers already using 5.25-inch floppy disks, that medium will remain popular for many years.

Consequently, most portable computer users need to be able to exchange information between the two disk sizes. Among the many ways of doing this are to have both diskdrives in your desktop system. There is probably the space and the necessary circuitry to install such a drive yourself. There are also some portables that will take the larger disks, or you can buy a separate plug-in accessory drive to enable your portable to use 5.25-inch disks.

For portable computing, the 3.5-inch disk will almost certainly be your prime removable storage medium. So you may well decide that the most cost-effective, hassle-free route to go is to standardize entirely on these. Convert all your data and programming on 5.25-inch floppies to 3.5-inch disks and stick with that format. You can do that easily with a range of transfer software programs. One of the most popular and easiest to use is Traveling Software's LapLink. It comes with cables that connect any two IBM-compatible personal computers and enables the information to flow freely and rapidly between them. The screen is split into two windows to show the files on each computer. There is a help menu only a keystroke away at any time.

The 3.5-inch microfloppies are coming in ever-increasing densities, but there are two main standards: 720K or 1.44MB. A kilobyte (K) is 1,024 bytes—each byte being eight bits of the binary code, with each bit the smallest unit of information a computer can recognize and the equivalent of an on or off switching instruction. A megabyte (MB) is 1,048,576 bytes—about a thousand kilobytes.

The 720K drives need double-sided, double-density disks, each side holding 360K in forty tracks. The high-density drives can store 720K in eighty tracks on each side of a double-sided, high-density disk. The disks look the same; often they are virtually identical except that the high-density has two small square holes in the corners of the bottom side, by the edge that is nearest to you when you insert the disk into the drive. (The hole with the sliding cover that both types of 3.5-inch disks have is used to write-protect the disk. A sensor in the drive will allow you to write on the disk only if the hole is covered.)

The extra hole at the other corner is used by the high-density drive to check if it is being fed a high-density disk. These cost a lot more than 720K disks, so some people use punches, drills, or the tips of soldering irons to make the hole in cheaper DD disks. This will usually fool a high-density drive into formatting the double-density disk, but it can be risky. Debris from making the hole can get into the disk and your drive and cause errors, even expensive damage to the drive mechanism. Also, the manufacturing quality standards for the double-density disk need not be as high as for the high-density, so you increase the risk of bad sectors and other problems that might cause loss of data. It's a cheapskate trick that is hardly worth the risk.

In theory, a laptop with a 1.44MB floppy drive should read any formatted disk to that standard and also those of the less dense 720K capacity. The main difference is that the heads for 1.44MB drives are thinner so they can read and write to a greater density. Consequently, reading the memory packed less tightly on a 720K disk should be easy. Usually it is, but because the tolerances are so tight, even a slight misalignment of the heads can make it difficult or impossible for one computer to read memory stored on a disk by another computer. The risk of failure increases when a 1.44MB drive tries to read a disk formatted at 720K or in another 1.44MB drive.

So your choice of format—as one parameter for your ideal system— will be influenced greatly by any need to exchange disks with other systems. It is far better to stick with one or the other. If you do have to interchange, get the highest quality disks available in each format and color code them—either the disks themselves or their labels—clearly identifying which is 720K and which 1.44MB.

Which is best? It's horses for courses. A portable that has only one or two floppy disk drives is more powerful and convenient if it uses 1.44MB high-density disks. However, since the disks are so small, so cheap, and most applications programs are supplied on 720K disks, these double-density disks are by no means outdated.

There is now such momentum behind the 3.5-inch format that it is benefiting from research and development to increase capacity and speed without sacrificing reliability. Chinon, one of the leading disk drive manufacturers, has launched a 4MB floppy disk drive that is only 1 inch high and weighs 440 grams; it can transfer data at nearly a megabit a second.

Another trend is to eliminate mechanical parts as much as possible to reduce size and battery consumption and increase reliability. So direct-drive motors in 3.5-inch disk drives, like those introduced by Epson, have superseded the use of belts. Belt-driven disk drives are becoming outdated, but there are still a lot of them around. If you have one and it gives you trouble, suspect the belt failing before you worry about expensive repairs and replacements.

Other variations of disk sizes and formats keep creeping into the portable marketplace. Each usually has some particular merit, but all are saddled with the problem of compatibility if you need to exchange data or programming. It's like French being a beautiful language, but a very restricted way of communicating if you are in an English-speaking country.

Hard disk drives are available the size of credit cards, and there are various types of removable storage media hailed as technological break-throughs in miniaturization and portability. However seductive the techno-logical progress, the applications are limited if the data stored in these various memory media are not readily accessible or transferable.

Hard (Fixed) Disks. Increasingly popular with portables is the hard disk, which is similar in concept to a stack of conventional floppies fixed inside a casing, yielding much greater memory that can be accessed far more quickly than a single floppy. The disks—platters, as they are called—inside a hard disk spin faster than a floppy; there are more of them and there are more read-write heads searching them.

A hard disk at least starts off being much faster to read from or write to than a single floppy, but as it fills up with programming and data, the

speed differential can narrow because of the FAT scattering data in empty
spaces, as we discussed earlier. If a file is divided into elements in various
parts of the disk that are some distance apart from each other, the
read-write head wastes time and battery power collecting them together
and then returning them as the file is changed and recommitted to memory.
To keep a hard disk functioning efficiently, you need to organize it into
directories and subdirectories, and use a utility program that will ensure
the memory storage is properly organized; otherwise, files will be split up
and stored in sectors all over the place and will take much longer to
retrieve.

In addition to adding bulk, weight, cost, and battery consumption to a
portable, a hard disk also adds risk. If your portable gets lost or damaged,
then so may your data on the hard drive. Although they are much faster
and hold a lot more memory, hard disks do have disadvantages. They are
essential for some portable computing tasks, but much of the work done on
the road can be undertaken just with floppies.

One option to provide secure backup data for vulnerable portable hard
disks is a separate streaming tape unit. Figure 7-1 shows the unit from
Weltec featuring data compression. It can contain up to 120 megabytes of
data.

The usual size of a hard disk drive for portables is either 20MB or
40MB, but they can go to over 100MB. To take full advantage of 286

Figure 7-1.   Separate streaming tape unit from Weltec.

or 386 systems, the bigger capacity drives are needed. It is always more cost-effective to overestimate the capacity you might require than to have to upgrade later. With a standard desktop you can exploit the competition that is bringing down the prices of hard drives you can install yourself. But the typical laptop is such a tight design that user modification is difficult or impossible.

Size is not the only measure of floppy disk or hard drive performance. Access time is important also. The read-write head should be able to get into position over the relevant sector of the disk's surface and extract the required information as quickly as the central processing unit can handle it.

- *Access time.* For the 8088 processors—those in the original PC and XT desktops and their portable equivalents—65 milliseconds (thousandths of a second) of hard disk access time is recommended; 40 milliseconds are needed for the AT equivalent, with an 80286 processor with a clock speed of 6 to 10 MHz; 30 milliseconds for the faster AT Turbo, with a clock speed of over 10MHz; and 30 milliseconds or faster for 386 systems, using the 80386 processor and having a clock speed of over 16MHz.
- *Clock speed.* Measured in millions of cycles per second, the clock speed is the speed at which the processor runs. Some 8088s or 80286s run faster than others, but an increased clock speed in itself will not help if the rest of the computer's electronics are not geared up to run at that speed. Watch out for this in portables from little-known makers.

Hard disks may be internal or external. The portable, external disk drives tend to be expensive because they are built to withstand a lot of movement. For example, the Shamrock unit is competitive in price and compact in size because the shock mounting is in a separate carrying case rather than on the drive assembly itself. The case also has a thin lead lining to protect data from airport X-rays—not necessarily a big risk in the United States but a more serious threat with higher radiation levels in security equipment in some overseas countries, or when there is repeated exposure. However fast, large, or powerful your portable's capacity to save memory, the data are so vulnerable that they are probably uninsurable. The only sure way to protect yourself against data loss is to have a braces-and-belt backup strategy, making extra copies of all important files, and storing them elsewhere. This is advisable for any computer user, but doubly so for anyone with important data on a portable's hard disk. A laptop with even a small-capacity hard disk can soon fill up with enough data that are more valuable, and cost more to recreate (if that is possible), than the computer itself.

Also, power down your portable in accordance with the maker's instructions before you move it. Don't just finish the job on hand, save the file, and throw the switch. If your system does not have automatic head parking, obtain a utility that automatically parks the read-write heads safely away from the surface of the hard disk at the end of a session so that the head is less likely to get jarred and thrown out of alignment when you move the computer. If the head is left up in the air, so to speak, it may crash into the disk if the computer is knocked or dropped.

Even if the computer falls out of a taxi, or is lost or stolen, your data are still safe if it is backed up onto floppy disks, a separate hard disk drive, tape, or other medium stored safely somewhere else.

Indeed, some portability enthusiasts assess their priorities and carry only their data from place to place, not their computers. In many situations, the hardware is proportionately cheap enough to ensure that duplicate systems are readily available in the places where they are likely to be needed.

There are signs of fundamental attitude changes starting among some experienced computer users who have always regarded hard disks as the key element for efficient, performance computing. The growing concern about computer crime and electronic vandalism—particularly in the form of viruses, worms, and other damaging programs—is giving a boost to the concept of the diskless personal computer, both desktop and portable.

The diskless workstations are networked to a central mini or mainframe computer that is subject to stringent security and controls. One of the main benefits is that the organization's data are far better protected than if reposing in the hard disks of a number of individual PCs, especially if they are traveling portables.

The days of the hard disk may be numbered by portable floppy storage systems of previously undreamed of capacity. Floppies of standard 3.5-inch physical size, but capable of holding about 3 million letters or digits, are now a reality. Under development in Japan are floppy systems capable of storing between 10 and 20 megabytes, ample for the great majority of portable applications. So it pays to keep up with what is happening in disk storage technology. Improvements are taking place that will have a major impact on portable computing. It is becoming far easier to approach your portable computing needs from the perspective of making the data portable, rather than the equipment on which to process it. Very high capacity disks provide a low-cost, extremely mobile form of memory of virtually limitless capacity.

Random Access Memory

RAM is a crucial measure of performance capability and has particular importance for the portable user. In fact, it is not really memory in the sense of disk storage we have examined already. Disks can provide a near-permanent means of storing data independently of the system. In contrast, RAM—an acronym for random access memory—is not for the long-term storage of data or programming codes, but a temporary repository of the data and codes currently being processed. It is the equivalent, for the computer, of the files that you take out of the filing cabinet and have on your desk while you work on a particular project.

RAM has limited space in which to contain the current information. A portable with only 120K of RAM is like a small desk that, because of its size, will seriously limit the tasks you can do on it. The bigger the RAM, the more efficiently you can work: all the data and programming instructions needed for the task will fit onto the desk. The more complex the task, the more likely you will need more data and codes than a RAM can hold. There is a considerable slowing down and loss of computing efficiency when that extra information has to be collected from the permanent memory on the hard or floppy disk. To make room for it, existing currently needed information must be overwritten, requiring another trip back to the files on disk when it is required again, perhaps a mere fraction of a second later.

RAM is very efficient. It has no moving parts. A grid of hundreds of thousands of transistors and other miniaturized electronic components forms a highly concentrated bank of memory cells within the RAM chips, of which there are usually eight in the typical PC system, with a ninth monitoring their activities. The bytes of data can be stored and retrieved in and out of those memory cells at speeds measured in millionths of a second, uninhibited by the physical limitations imposed by a read-write head moving over the surface of a fixed or floppy disk.

So RAM is also economical in battery power. There is no physical action to drain energy, and RAM can be made much smaller than a disk system, which requires physical movement. Microprocessor chips are also inherently more robust than any mechanical device in withstanding the rigors of travel.

Because of the speed with which RAM works, a growing trend in computing—and one particularly appropriate for portable users—is to have useful programs in RAM-resident form. They are loaded into the RAM chips and stay there all the time the computer is running, ready to be called up the moment they are needed. The software that monitors the state of your portable's battery is a RAM-resident program. Many portables now have sophisticated monitoring procedures running from RAM that will switch down functions to conserve battery power. The backlighting for the screen should certainly turn off if there has been no keyboard activity for some time.

The new versions of applications programs tend to need more RAM because they are more powerful. They can run faster by grabbing the information they need quickly from the RAM chips rather than having to go back to the much slower disk drives to retrieve everything.

So RAM is getting very crowded. We have the equivalent of working at a desk onto which more files keep getting dumped, until eventually some fall to the floor, others get in the way of each other, and productivity is reduced.

There are some software tricks that will help, especially devices such as RAM disks, caches, print spoolers, and the like, which can stretch the RAM available into a supplementary section that the operating system normally reserves for housekeeping purposes.

However, memory in general and random access memory in particular are the main restrictions on computer performance. Get the biggest RAM you can, because it doesn't add significantly to the bulk or weight of your portable, although it will push the price up because chips are expensive, particularly those with faster access speeds.

RAM Drive. If you have spare space in a capacious RAM, then you have the immediate capability of adding the equivalent of another super-efficient disk drive to your computer without spending a cent. This is a simulated disk called a RAM disk, a RAM drive, or a virtual disk. You give it a letter like any other drive; it could be your B drive if you have only one floppy drive, the C drive if you have two floppies, or the D drive if you already have a hard disk called C.

You use this RAM drive as if it were a mechanical drive, copying files and programs to it and working on them there with the best speed your system is capable of delivering. However, the files must be copied back to the floppy or hard drives for long-term storage because RAM memory is totally dependent on having power to remember what has been loaded into it. If your batteries run down or you switch off—or someone walks past and catches the lead from your adapter, which can so easily detach from its socket—then everything on the RAM drive is lost.

A RAM drive can be created directly with DOS commands if you have version 3.0 or higher. You can make this an automatic operation incorporated in the batch files brought up as you boot the system, or you

Figure 7-2.   Stages in which the memory of the Compaq SLT/286 can be expanded.

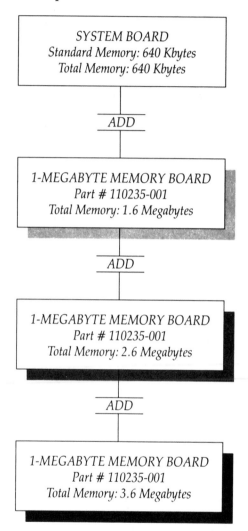

can load a particular application for which a RAM disk is useful. Your DOS manual details what is possible for your version and portable system; some portables now have automatic RAM drives, or their equivalents in the form of memory caches.

Adding Memory. Of course, you cannot create a RAM drive unless there is sufficient space in RAM to accommodate it. That can prove impossible, because just one RAM-hungry applications program (or a less demanding one having to share space with several RAM-resident utilities) can consume all the available space. DOS itself imposes a limit of 640K of RAM that can be used in the conventional way by applications programs, but memory performance can be extended and expanded by additional chips, boards, and software, depending on the system.

Figure 7-2 is a flowchart showing the stages in which the memory of the Compaq SLT/286 laptop can be expanded from the original 640K RAM through to a maximum of 3.6MB. (1MB should cope with most DOS program requirements, but 2MB are required for OS/2.)

The RAM in most portables is either difficult, expensive, or impossible to expand, whereas a conventional desktop PC is built with an easily removed case and room inside for modification. So you need to get your RAM needs worked out before purchasing most portable hardware—yet another reason to start the selection process by deciding first what you need to do and only then making decisions about hardware.

Buffer Memory. A form of RAM that can be manipulated to advantage on a portable is buffer memory. Information flows in and out of RAM as much as fifty times faster than to and from a disk, so the operating system keeps some information in a RAM buffer. Then, when the applications program needs something from the disk—a spell check, for example—DOS will try to hold at least part of that in a buffer where it can be grabbed easily and quickly without searching the disk for it.

It would seem logical that the more buffers available, the better. But buffers consume memory and work more efficiently with some diskdrives and applications programs than with others. It may actually take longer in some cases for the computer to search through its RAM buffers than to go straight to the disk.

DOS will adjust the numbers of buffers it creates according to the size of your system's RAM and its disk capacity. It will only create two buffers for a system with 360K disk drives and a mere 128K RAM memory, or fifteen buffers if you have 512K or more. Your particular hardware and software combination might work more efficiently with twenty or more buffers, especially if you have a later version of DOS. Later DOS programs do a better job of buffer management than earlier ones. They also enable buffers to be created in expanded memory, making very good use of this added capacity, but at the possible risk of your buffer modifications creating conflict with certain programs.

Buffers are easy to write. The DOS instruction is simply BUFFERS = (the number of buffers you require). You can have as many as 999 buffers in MS-DOS 4.0. But, like setting the ignition timing or fuel mixture on your car, achieving the most desirable tuning for your situation can get complicated. Consult your DOS and system manuals, and follow recommendations given by the publishers of your applications program.

It pays to experiment. You can tune a car by advancing the ignition in small steps until the engine pings, and then back off a little. Similarly, you can tune your system for a particular applications program by increasing the number of buffers in steps of four or five until the program's performance stops improving and starts deteriorating. Then you need to go back slightly to the optimum setting.

Read Only Memory

ROM—read only memory—is memory contained in a different kind of chip. It is actually software converted into permanent electronic circuitry. Unlike RAM, the memory in ROM cannot be changed by the average computer user, but the payoff is that it survives without electrical power, ready for action again as soon as you switch the computer back on or the batteries are recharged. The instructions and data contained in a ROM chip are, for all practical purposes, there for good.

Portables with their operating systems, and even some applications programs built into the hardware in the form of ROM, can be a mixed blessing. At first sight, it seems great having DOS, a word processor, a spell checker, and other applications packed into ROM chips inside your portable. This eliminates the need for the software on separate floppy disks, which take up a lot of the RAM memory when the computer is running. However, your portable computer is most likely to become outdated quicker by improvements in the software programs you need than by advances in the hardware. You have to live with the original versions of programs in ROM, unless you are able to update by physically swapping chips, which can be expensive and difficult, even impossible if the chips are soldered into place, a common practice in manufacturing portables.

Becoming increasingly important for portables is greater use of PROM—programmable read only memory—which is the form of permanent memory chips that customers can program. EPROM—the E stands for erasable—are PROM chips that users can erase and change. Special equipment and expertise is required. These are more applicable to corporate portable systems.

CD-ROM

This is an exciting memory medium with enormous potential for portable users. Nothing yet matches CD-ROM's ability to get so much information into such a compact, practical, and readily transportable form. The medium was restricted during the 1980s, but the growth now taking place was symbolized by the Encyclopaedia Britannica organization in 1990, when it issued *Compton's Encyclopedia* on just one disk the same size and appearance as the popular compact discs for music.

So you can hold in the palm of your hand the equivalent of twenty-six hefty books containing nearly 9 million words, some 15,000 pictures, plus 45 animated sequences, and audio recordings of some of the world's most renowned music and speeches by historical figures.

Lawyers are an obvious professional sector to make good use of portable computers able to process data stored on CD-ROM disks. A whole law library can be contained in a briefcase; there has never been such a practical medium for archiving case reports and accessing them by simple key word searches.

However, CD-ROM has been handicapped by conflicting standards, different methods of storing and searching records, and other incompatibility problems. The hardware also has been overpriced and, with a few notable exceptions, slow to be integrated into portable systems. A leader was CD Technology Inc., with the first complete portable office in one box, including a CD unit that could enable a doctor to listen to his favorite music while accessing the *Physicians' Desk Reference* to prepare treatment procedures he could then fax to his patient or the hospital.

CD-ROM drives have been most easily and economically incorporated in lunchbox portables like the unit from PC-Brand, available by mail order at very keen pricing.

This unit is another example of the advantages of the lunchbox style for a portable computer, despite the tendency for experts to deride it because it is not on the cutting edge of miniaturization.

CD-ROM is becoming available in more compact hardware, notably the Scenario Dynabook, which has an integral CD-ROM drive. Just the drive and the disk in it provide memory and the means of accessing it equivalent to a 3.5-inch floppy drive with over 800 of the 720K standard disks!

The range of plug-in external CD-ROM drives is increasing steadily and prices are falling rapidly. Most computers will run CD-ROM units because they are not dependent on CPU capacity or performance. The software choices are expanding also, and we can expect more enterprising packaging of fully integrated programs. Microsoft Office was the first example of this, combining on one CD the powerful Word, Excel, Powerpoint, and Mail applications, plus all their manuals, clip art, templates, and other useful software. In their original packages, these would take up much of the space in your car trunk. Now they can go into your pocket.

Central Processing Units

The other major performance rating given to portables relates to their central processing units (CPUs) and associated electronics that control and execute the actual data processing work. The performance and power image of a DOS personal computer is very much linked to the Intel microprocessor model number at the heart of its CPU.

Models 8088 and the 8086 are now at the bottom of the scale. They are the microprocessor workhorses dating from 1978, the beginning of the personal computer revolution. The 8088, used in the first IBM-PC and XT models and their clones, is slow by today's standards because it cycles information in eight-bit groups, each constituting a byte or single character.

The 8086 was a significant step forward because it handled sixteen-bit groups through sixteen-bit data buses, the internal highways of the computer. They could cope with a greater volume of information traffic moving faster than the eight-bit bus. But the speed of data processing is also related to clock speed and other factors (see earlier section on hard disks). So there are Turbo PCs, the equivalent of autos with souped-up engines, giving a boost in operating speed that augments the performance of the 8088 considerably, perhaps more cost-effective in some applications than the improved performance that the 8086 achieves.

The 80286 dates from 1984 and is an Intel chip introduced with the IBM AT, meaning Advanced Technology. With its sixteen-bit system, the 80286 microprocessor can be twenty times faster in some respects than the 8088, with lots of scope for tweaking its performance for various applications. A 286 computer will run all the programs created for the PC and XT, plus software written to exploit its greater performance capabilities. Graphics programs, for example, are much better suited to 286 systems, but there is still a good selection of well-refined graphics programs that will run on 8088 systems, especially when one considers the screen and other limitations of doing graphics on a portable.

The 386 portables are the Thunderbird powerhouses that use the Intel 80386 central processing unit, which has 275,000 transistors—ten times more than the 8088. It also represents a significant increase in the volume and speed of information traffic it can handle by having thirty-two-bit bus capability. The 386 can achieve a doubling again of the processing speed of the 286, and it is much more able to handle several tasks at the same time. The difference between 286 and 386 performance is not as small as some advertisers for 286 portables would try to make you believe. On the other hand, the increase may be performance you will not be able to put to good use, just as the typical American family does not need the eight-cylinder gas-guzzling motors that Detroit put into our autos during the 1970s.

There is an 80386SX microprocessor that adds to the confusion. It is a slower, not faster, sixteen-bit variation of the 386—a halfway house upgrade for 286 desktops. Auto manufacturers slot such variants into market niches between their main model ranges. The 386SX has significant advantages over the 286, but the 386 will be the chip that sets the pace in the portable computing environment of the 1990s. Moving in from the wings and starting to play specialist roles at the top end of the field is the 80486, a faster derivative of the 386.

There are also families of 68000 and 88000 microprocessors from Motorola that Apple and other manufacturers use, but the DOS world is dominated by the Intel 8088 and its successors.

In summary, remember that the performance curve rises significantly with each succeeding generation, but increased performance is only of value if it is in a form that fits your particular computing needs. Also, no computer system can be any faster than its slowest component—that may be the clock speed, the CPU, or you, the user. As Mahatma Gandhi emphasized, speed is not everything. His wise words are quoted at the beginning of this book to emphasize that speed is often not relevant to getting the most benefit from portable computing, or from life.

8

Peripherals: Work-to-Go Accessories

There is an ever-expanding list of peripheral equipment to make portable computers more productive on the road. Here are the features to look for in the most useful work-to-go accessories.

Printers

The personal computer was supposed to herald the era of the paperless office. That hasn't happened. Indeed, the paper avalanche has escalated as computing has become widespread. Old habits die hard, and when it really comes to the crunch, we still do not have sufficient confidence in electronic data storage to trust it completely. Also, there remain many situations in which hard copies are more convenient and practical because electronic data processing has to interface with the still paper dominated business world.

Do You Need a Printer at All?

There are many situations on the road when it may seem you need to print out hard copies. In fact, you may be able to overcome that need in other ways. If we really reappraise our work styles, portable computing may get us far closer to the paperless office than we have been able to achieve at our desks.

For example, electronic mail can eliminate a great deal of paper. Exchanging disks or sending documents by modem is faster and usually more economical than transferring the information in hard-copy form. Most of the reference material we need can be handled more efficiently when it is computerized. We are being encouraged to do this increasingly, as portable computing demonstrates that information can be both captured and used far more flexibly than hiding it in stacks of paper.

After some practice—and gaining the required confidence—you may well find that you can function very well on the road without making printed copies of work you perform on your portable. It is rather like learning to ride a cycle with trainer wheels, or swimming with buoyancy aids. The transition to riding or swimming free is traumatic at first, but then you wonder why you ever needed the props at all. That is much the same with computer printouts. Gain proficiency in handling information electronically, and much of the paper you think is essential soon becomes redundant.

There is an excellent type of software utility that acts as the training wheels during this transition. It is so useful you will want to keep it around as an integral part of your portable system.

Print spoolers, or virtual print buffers, take the output that you want to print into hard copy and line it up for its turn on the printer. Then you move on to your next task, rather than wait for the printer to finish its work and hand back the use of your computer to you. Spoolers are a common feature of networks, in which several terminals share a printer.

You can use the same principle with your portable to good effect. Create your documents and store them in sequence on a disk, set up as if they were to emerge as paper copies from a printer. You can use a simple data-compression program to make hundreds of pages fit easily onto a single double-density disk. Instead of carrying around a pile of paper, just search through the disk when you need to refer to your documents. It is particularly convenient in difficult working situations such as on an aircraft.

When—or if—you do need a hard copy, you can run the spooled output on a printer when you get back to base. Chances are you will find that your need to have hard copies steadily reduces as you become more proficient and more confident at working without paper.

PrintRite is a 50K terminate-and-stay resident software program that fools your portable into thinking it is hooked up to a printer. It "prints" your reports and other documentation rapidly to disk in compressed form and either holds them there like a sheaf of electronic papers or manages their printing in the conventional way, without delaying use of the computer. You can shuffle and rearrange the documents however you wish before they are committed to paper—if they ever are.

Printing Options on the Road

Of course, there are situations on the road in which hard copies are essential but you cannot borrow a printer. Then the only valid option is to carry your own printer with you. (One trick when you must have a hard copy and you are stuck in a hotel without a printer is to send yourself a fax from your portable. Within minutes, the operator will call you to let you know that your printout is waiting for collection and delivery to your room!)

Portable printers are now very good—and can be a lot better if you know a few road-warrior tricks in using them.

Match the printer to your needs. Some will run on readily available, standard disposable battery cells or nicads that can be shared with other equipment you are carrying with you. If not, you will have to lug along a usually bulky and heavy adapter or charger especially for the printer.

Some models use thermal paper—specially coated stock like fax paper that is expensive and does not yield very good quality. These may be all right if you need the hard copies for your own purposes, but they aren't likely to impress clients. Also, some of the dot matrix, thermal-transfer, and ink-jet plain paper printers for portables fall well below the quality of desktop laser or daisywheel printers.

Some printers require special coated paper, and all give better results on a smooth-coated paper stock than ordinary bond. The paper sold for laser printers often gives good results. Most paper has a right and a wrong side for printing—one side takes the ink far more efficiently than the other. The packaging usually indicates which is the right side, or you may be able to tell by touch, or by holding the paper up to the light and reading the watermark, if there is one. The side facing you when you can read the watermark correctly is the best side for printing.

Book paper, unlike bond, will print to equal standards on either side, and you may find that you prefer to take this type on the road with you, selecting the most suitable after experimenting.

If you must make hard copies on preprinted letterhead, you may experience difficulty getting a good output on the textured papers often used to enhance corporate images. If you cannot change the company stationery, consider creating a version of it on disk that you can call up and print as required. It could be a special version that you update with the time and place where the document is originated, adding interest and immediacy that may more than compensate for your portable printer's inadequacies. Heading a business letter from your mobile office on Flight 366 out of Miami can give a sense of immediacy and impress the recipient more than immaculate correspondence on a three-color embossed letter-head on linen paper!

A fuzzy image lacking in contrast can often be improved by photo-copying it, especially if you can reduce the size so that the dots on the original become less obvious and the contrast is enhanced.

You may also be able to improve the appearance of on-the-road documents by preprinting at least part of them, perhaps in color. Both image and productivity can be enhanced by producing more work on forms of various kinds. You create the forms using the excellent software available for this, and print them up crisply and professionally on the office laser printer. The information to go onto the forms can be prepared on the portable, using a stored formatting, so that when they are printed out the data fit neatly into the allocated spaces on the form. Then the less-than-great dot matrix or ink-jet text will not matter.

The situations in which this works well are many. Advertising account executives and consultants can generate their client contact reports. Sales-people can apply the technique to preparing orders or quotations.

Available Models

The most popular portable printer for years has been the Diconix, taken over and developed by Kodak (Figure 8-1). Weighing under five pounds, it is about the size of a paperback novel and fits easily into most briefcases, leaving enough room for a laptop also.

The Diconix used to require special paper to give the best results, but Kodak improved the ink formulation for a new generation of models for the 1990s that yield far better output on ordinary paper. If you have an older Diconix, try one of the new ink cartridges and it may give your printer a new lease of life.

Toshiba and other manufacturers have increased the range of portable printers available, as with their 24-pin portable Toshiba Expresswriter 311.

You can now get portable printers that will cope well with virtually all on-the-road hard-copy needs, including handling either single sheets or fanfold form paper with almost equal dexterity. They can produce over-head transparencies and a wide range of font styles and graphics.

But to get the best out of any printer, your software must be properly set up for it. Make sure your applications programs are configured appropriately and be prepared to experiment. If particular software does not yield satisfactory hard-copy output, contact the publisher or the printer manufacturer's technical support services, because they may well have a quick and easy fix.

Modems

A modem can be the most useful accessory for your portable computer—far more so than a printer. It is a small but complex electronic device that translates digital data in the electronic form used by the computer into modulated audio frequency signals that can be transmitted over telephone lines, or via radio links such as those used by cellular phones.

There are two types of modem hardware: internal and external. An

Figure 8-1. The Kodak Diconix 150 Plus.

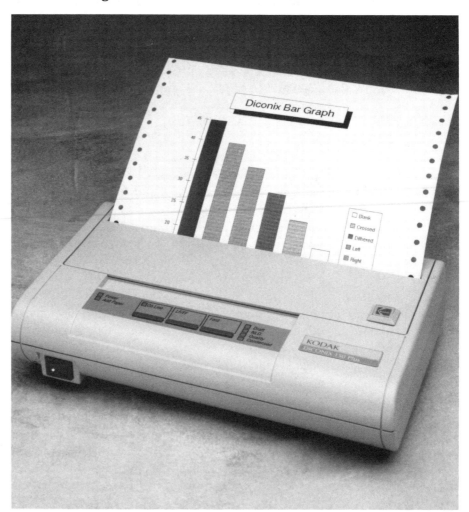

internal modem has the electronics contained on a board that fits snugly inside the portable computer. You buy the computer with the modem included, or in some cases can add an internal modem from either the computer manufacturer or a third-party vendor.

The Toshiba internal modem is unusual in meeting most international needs. Users who roam the world are often better off with an external modem, because standards for telecommunications differ greatly from country to country. In some places the telephone circuits are so poor that the faster transmission rates of 1200, 2400, and 9600 baud that work fine in the United States or Europe may result in garble in some African, South American, and Asian territories.

So a plug-in external modem may give more flexibility and control in unusual situations.

The fact that an external modem can have an independent power supply means that it is not a drain on the computer's batteries. The cost is probably lower than for an internal modem of equivalent performance, while being able to see the status lights helps in monitoring what is going on and identifying problems in tricky communications situations. On the negative side, an external modem is another piece of equipment to carry around, the inconvenience aggravated by the wires dangling from it.

Baud Rate

The baud rate quoted for modems is the measure in bits per second of the speed with which it will transmit and receive data. You may need to transmit as slowly as 300 baud to send a file over a bad telephone or radio link, but usually in developed countries the 2400- or 9600-baud rates work fine and will save you a lot of time and money. For most business users, 1200 baud is now a reasonable minimum; 2400 is much better for all practical purposes and will soon repay the initial higher cost.

If you do much communicating under difficult situations, consider a modem using the Microcom Networking Protocol (MNP), which incorporates advanced error monitoring and will adjust the baud rate to the conditions of the line. However, the modems at both ends must be able to handle MNP to enjoy these advantages. You can also get modems and fax transmission/receiving circuitry combined on the same board or in the same external package.

Accompanying Equipment

Communications software is needed in addition to the modem hardware. Most modems have special programs of their own, but you may

prefer to use the communications module of an integrated software package or established programs such as Procomm, the universal shareware communications program.

Other equipment for communications on the road may be necessary to overcome the obstacles that hotels and telephone companies put in your way. There should be no problems if the phone from which you wish to transmit or receive has a standard jack into which your modem will connect directly. Unfortunately, many hotels have nonstandard jacks, or the telephone cable disappears through a plate in the wall and you cannot get to the socket at all.

Those situations require the appropriate combination of converters, plugs, and leads to make the connection. In some cases, you have to unscrew the plate in the wall to locate the standard modular plug concealed inside. Or you may have to unscrew the mouthpiece of the receiver and hook up directly to the leads with alligator clips.

The easiest way to prepare for any eventuality is to get a kit of plugs, extension cable, adapters, clips, and other useful items. The Road Warrior Deluxe Toolkit should help you cope with any modem-communications situation in any hotel or motel in the United States.

If you need to transmit data from a public telephone, an acoustic coupler is the way to go. It fits over the mouthpiece and earpiece to send and receive audio signals directly, without electrical connection from the phone to the computer. You can get these from Radio Shack or mail order suppliers who specialize in portable computing needs.

Portable Fax

It is now easy and inexpensive to add the ability to send and receive documents by facsimile transmission to almost any portable computer system. The computer already contains much of the electronics needed for a fax. You can add the rest in the form of a plug-in board. Some cost under $200, but they may not fit into a portable or may consume so much power that they will quickly run down the battery.

Trying to send graphics or any substantial amount of text can gobble up memory very rapidly, so if your portable is to be used for fax purposes, a hard disk may be essential. Prepare also for slow, slow production on your portable printer of hard copies of faxes containing graphics.

Using fax boards and portable fax machines is also more time-consuming and difficult than you are probably used to with office fax

machines. You may be better off sending and receiving the equivalent of faxes via an electronic mail service such as MCI mail (see Appendix C). You can send a document to the service direct from your word processing software and it will be delivered as a fax to the addressee. The process works in reverse for faxes being sent to you; you pick them up by modem along with other electronic mail.

Despite its snags, the fax on a board—as an external accessory for your computer or as a stand-alone unit—can be a great productivity boon on the road and will add a whole new dimension to portable computing. The first step is to check if your portable has the internal space and the memory capabilities to accommodate a fax board. Many come on half-boards, occupying the short slots, so don't despair if you have insufficient room for a full board. If space is too tight for an internal board, consider the external portable fax units.

If you want to fax graphics or other visuals, you will need to either create them in the computer or scan them in. A trick if you are traveling without a scanner is to get the visual faxed into your portable, so that it arrives in a digitized form. It can be easier to send a faxed visual from the hotel lobby to the laptop in your room than to carry a scanner on trips. Faxing could also be the most convenient way to get the corporate logo into your computer so that you can use it on documents.

Faxing photographs is not feasible with most portables because the scales of gray consume so much memory. Nor can you expect to use lots of fancy fonts, or to manipulate the texts that you receive as if they had already been converted into codes your word processing software can use. It is not feasible, for example, to use a fax-to-computer link as a substitute for character recognition hardware and software.

Although bulkier and more expensive, the best route for many users to acquire faxing capabilities on the road is to have a stand-alone portable fax. One of the many compact and attractively priced desktop faxes that run on conventional AC power may be sufficiently portable for your needs and can be run from a battery via a converter.

A recent development is the dedicated paperless fax, which works with both Mac and MS-DOS systems. This Ricoh unit pioneered the new approach in 1990. It can send and receive faxes independently of the computer, holding up to fourteen pages in its 512K buffer memory. Consequently, the interruption to other work when sending or receiving faxes is minimized. Indeed, the computer does not have to be on at all to enable you to send or receive documents, because the paperless fax can be left on standby waiting for an incoming call.

Figure 8-2.   Ricoh's MC-50 portable copier/digitizer scanner.

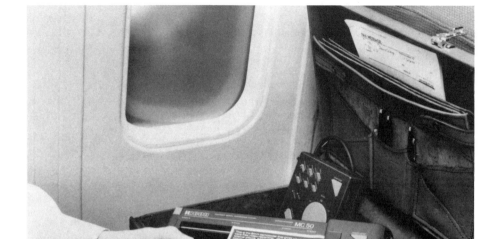

Combination Units

The first comprehensive solution to portable information capture, copying, and transmission was also introduced by Ricoh. Called the Portable Digital Information System, it has three modular units that interact with each other: a portable copier, an image controller and scanner, and a facsimile interface.

The copier, unlike other hand-held portable copiers, scans the original without having to be rolled over it. However, the image size is small: only 3⅞ by 6½ inches, the metric A6 paper size. Add the image controller and scanner and the image can be enlarged, reduced, and otherwise manipulated within the limits of the paper size, or loaded into the computer for processing like other graphics.

Add the facsimile transmitter-receiver and you can send the scanned image as a fax, or receive faxed images and process them. There is a

version of the controller for Macintosh users to give them on-the-road document handling that exceeds what most of us have on our desktops. It might be the only scanning and faxing facility you need.

Of course, by clever combination of an ordinary hand scanner—now discounted for well under $200—a portable printer, and a portable computer with a fax modem you can create a flexible system that will meet most portable office requirements at a reasonable price.

Figure 8-2 shows Ricoh's MC-50 portable copier/digitizer scanner. It has been described as an office in a briefcase. When used with Ricoh's IM-A image controller/scanner, the MC-50 has the capacity to store graphics files in IBM-PC compatibles or Macintosh computers for desktop publishing. The MC-50 is also useful for copying notes, documents, books, and rare and fragile papers. It can also be used with Ricoh's IM-F portable facsimile transceiver.

9

Power to the System

The life-force of portable computers and their peripherals is electrical energy. The availability of that energy is a dominant factor in where and how the system can be used. Creative use of the many alternatives already available can be more important than new battery technology in extending your portable computing horizons. Desktop Macintoshes and IBM PCs and clones are being run off car batteries and solar and wind-power generators around the world, from California to the heart of Africa. The sun, the wind, and the imagination are extending the power capacities of portables everywhere.

Ironically, surveys repeatedly show that in conventional business applications portables are used as much as 95 percent of the time either connected to or within easy reach of electrical outlets. But look at some of the alternatives to relying on standard batteries and adapters, and the opportunities for working anywhere become apparent.

Even if your computing needs are best met by the most powerful portable or desktop that will only run on main AC current, you can still make your computing portable. Adding mobility to a desktop computer, some of which are now very compact, can be the most cost-effective solution in many situations. Remember, however, that desktop machines are not built to be moved around frequently, and the cost savings you achieve by pressing a static desktop into a wandering life-style could yield early unreliability problems. Hard disks are the components that travel least well. Before moving any computer with a hard disk it is wise to park the heads, a facility usually packaged with the popular utilities programs.

The original Macs travel well, are compact, even come complete with a handle and a range of optional travel bags. They have some of the characteristics of portable computers, are available second-hand quite cheaply (certainly a lot less than the new generations of Macintosh and Mac clone portables), and can be connected to external power sources not dependent on household or office current.

Batteries

Any personal computer and its peripherals can be run in virtually any location from a wide range of external power sources, including sun, wind, and water. We will look at those options later. First, let's take a quick tour of the types of batteries you are most likely to encounter in portable computing, so that you can assess which is most appropriate for your needs and how to get the best performance from it. Battery performance is only partly a factor of its type and design; much depends on how each is used—or abused.

If battery performance is particularly important in your computer application, the rapid advances being made in battery technology may be the single most important reason for your wanting to upgrade your machine. On the other hand, I have some alternatives that may avoid the need for an expensive upgrade.

There are some attractive cost-saving benefits possible if you are well informed about batteries and alternative power sources for computers. Many models become obsolete and so are deeply discounted simply because their battery performances are no longer competitive. These can be excellent buys if the other characteristics of the computer are acceptable. The best buys of all can be little-used computers sold second-hand because they no longer work properly, but which are only suffering temporary and easily remedied ill health because of battery problems. The performance of a battery can be drastically reduced by bad user practices and often restored by fairly simple procedures that we will look at.

Types of Batteries

Your computer, printer, and other portable equipment will be powered by two basic types of battery: primary or secondary cells. The primary type are disposables—you use them until they are discharged and then you throw them away. The secondary cells are rechargeable.

Although you may well have had contact with only one specific type of battery, the others are of more than passing interest because they may provide alternative ways of powering your computer and its peripherals. That applies whether you have a notebook or pocket computer, a bigger laptop or transportable, or want to make a desktop system mobile. Learning the characteristics of the different batteries may influence how you work. Indeed, it may help you assess what tasks can become portable. Just a little advance planning and battery management can make a big difference to your computing productivity and convenience.

Much equipment will accept either primary or secondary cells—for example, the pocket computers and most of the portable printers—but don't mix them at the same time because the chemical reactions by which disposable and rechargeable cells create electricity are distinctly different. Also different is the way they discharge, and this can be important in the functioning of your equipment. Mixing primary and secondary cells—even if they look identical except for the labeling—usually results in lowered performance and can even cause damage, such as leakage of chemicals that will harm delicate electronic components.

Also, do not mix new cells with those that are partly discharged, except in situations where there is no alternative. The discharged cell will tend to drain the others quickly, shortening their useful life. When using secondary batteries a lot, especially if rotating several sets of rechargeable cells, it is easy to lose track of which are new or recharged and which are run down. You can create a simple monitoring system by applying sticky tape, or those adhesive write-protect tabs supplied with floppy disks, to mark new or fully charged batteries. A small voltameter or battery tester, readily available at around $10 or less from Radio Shack or other electronics stores, will both identify the charged from the flat batteries and also identify those not performing to specification. A malfunctioning cell in a set will drain its neighbors and reduce the efficiency of all the batteries.

If you get the full life out of your laptop that you should, then the battery may well be the first major component that requires replacing. If cost is not significant, the easiest way is to have it replaced by an authorized dealer. But most portables have batteries that are designed to be changed by the average user, and this should be a simple task if you follow carefully the directions in the manual.

Some computers are designed so that the battery pack is easily detachable. This feature is essential if you are likely to be heavily dependent on integral battery power and need to carry a spare with you. Others are not intended to be taken out frequently and will be under a cover that has to be unscrewed (see Figure 9-1).

Figure 9-1. Battery cover removal.

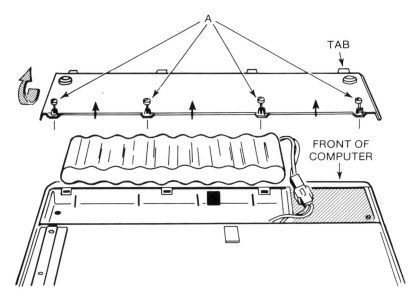

To save money when replacing a battery pack or a faulty cell, take it to a comprehensive electronics store. You may get a generic replacement at substantially less than the official dealer price. But make sure that the dimensions, location, type of connections, and other features are an exact match.

Eventually even the larger laptops will have batteries that last for the life of the machine, with long intervals between recharging. While conventional batteries will run down at the rate of about 30 percent a month even if you do not use them, the new polymer batteries lose as little as 1 percent and produce five times as much power as existing nicads and lead-acid cells of about the same weight and size.

Disposable Batteries

Carbon-Zinc Batteries. The most popular—and cheapest—primary cells are 1.5-volt carbon-zinc batteries. They are used in nearly all pocket and notebook computers, most portable printers, and in radios and flashlights. About half of the billions of 1.5-volt cells sold are AA size; about 40 percent of the market goes to the larger C and D sizes; while the smaller AAA size, together with the square 9-volt cell, make up most of the remaining battery sales.

The carbon-zinc cell has been evolving for over a century and can be found all over the world under various brand names.

The metal container of the cell is made from zinc and forms the negative electrode. It is usually covered by a plastic, metal, or paper jacket as an outer shield. Inside, making up the bulk and weight of the cell, is the positive electrode. In standard carbon-zinc cells this will be a compound of carbon black and natural manganese dioxide ore, while more expensive premium cells—often labeled "heavy duty" or some similar description—probably use zinc chloride. The positive terminal is the rod running through the center of the battery.

This type of cell, as with the vast majority of all batteries used in computers and other consumer electronic equipment, is of the closed type. A chemical reaction takes place inside the cell, in which ions flow between the negative and positive electrodes. This internal reaction is converted into external electrical power in the form of electrons to meet the demands from the electrical circuit into which the cell is connected.

The quality of materials and manufacture exert a big influence on how much performance you can expect from carbonizing cells. Inferior ones discharge themselves more quickly, severely limiting their life, and may well be prone to leaking with the risk of damaging your equipment. The heavy-duty or high-performance claims of little-known brands may be no more than creative labeling, while in some parts of the world there is extensive counterfeiting of popular brands, so you risk buying a cheap, inferior cell with a premium-brand name on it.

In batteries, you tend to get very much what you pay for and bargains should be suspect. Deeply discounted batteries are often old stock that have deteriorated in storage. Most manufacturers do not date-stamp their batteries, so about the only way to be reasonably sure of getting fresh stock is to buy from an outlet with a substantial turnover that makes it unlikely a battery has sat for a long time in the warehouse or on the store shelf.

Alkaline Batteries. The next step up the social scale of batteries is the alkaline cell, which looks virtually the same from the outside but is very different in construction.

Although more expensive, the superior performance of the alkaline cell almost always makes it a better choice than the carbon-zinc cell. Using alkaline cells may actually reduce the operating cost of your equipment because they not only tend to last longer but also maintain their voltage better throughout their working life.

The steel and plastic outer casings of the alkaline battery much reduce the risk of leakage. The negative electrode inside is made of powdered zinc, which gives a much greater surface area for a more efficient chemical reaction. More expensive electrolytic manganese dioxide instead of a natural ore is used for the positive electrode, and this enhances performance also.

Lithium Batteries. Your equipment may also use mercury and silver oxide, or lithium, primary cells. These are usually encountered in a thin button shape, like the lithium battery powering your computer's internal clock or preserving your backup memory.

Although comparatively expensive, these cells generate considerable electrical power in proportion to their size and have a long life under normal circumstances. The mercury cells are usually the cheapest and give more energy in terms of their volume than the silver oxide cells, which have the edge in energy output in proportion to weight and in their performance at low temperatures.

Lithium cells of different types have been subjected to intensive research and development, and they will become increasingly important in all portable electronic applications. Much of the research initiative has come as a result of their use in military equipment, so we will all benefit from a vast effort to increase the performance of lithium cells.

Rechargeable Batteries

Secondary—or rechargeable—cells and batteries are used in all kinds of portable computing equipment. They may be in the same external format as the primary cells we have just examined, or be put together in various combinations to form batteries and battery packs that vary greatly between equipment manufacturers.

Many battery packs are not interchangeable between different brands of computers—often not even between different models from the same manufacturer. So replacements for these customized secondary batteries can be very expensive and can sometimes be difficult to obtain. If, for example, you are choosing a portable from a small manufacturer who might not be around when your battery needs replacing, it is wise to make sure the battery pack is of a widely used configuration obtainable from other sources.

There are two main types of secondary rechargeable cells: nickel-cadmium and lead-acid. Nickel-cadmium has dominated the electronic equipment field, but the potential of new generations of lead-acid batteries was given a big boost by the use of this type in the first of the Macintosh portables. So it is worth examining both in some detail.

Nickel-Cadmium Batteries. The nickel-cadmium cell, or nicad (see Figure 9-2), is far more complex and consequently more expensive than primary cells because it has to accommodate a reversal of the electrical energy-generating chemical reaction. Over a billion nicads are sold every year, most going directly to equipment manufacturers to be incorporated in cordless phones, computers, and other appliances. Although more expensive, the nicads tend not to deliver as much performance as an equivalent disposable cell, and this may be a factor in your buying decisions.

The positive and negative electrodes are made from metal plates of nickel and cadmium, respectively, fastened together in a sandwich of steel reinforcement and plastic separator sheets into a long strip. This strip is then either wound into a tube or folded to fit into the cell's nickel-plated steel case. The negative plate is connected to the cell's steel case and the

Figure 9-2.   Sealed nickel-cadmium cell.

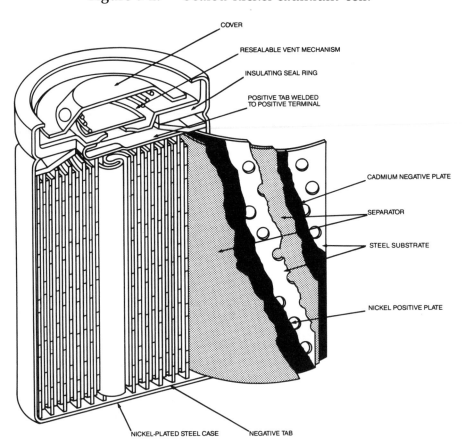

positive plate to the terminal on the top cover. Just before the case and cover are joined, enough potassium hydroxide electrolyte is injected to wet the plates.

When the battery is discharged or recharged, gases are formed inside that should recombine with the elements within the cell and cause no problems. However, excessive overcharging—and even some instances of very deep discharge—can build up excessive pressure that will blow the vent and the battery will not function properly. To minimize the risk of this, batteries should be recharged with a system designed specifically for them, which in most cases will have some preventive overcharging circuitry built in. The maximum time limits for charging should be followed also.

Training Your Battery to Give Its Best

Your recharging habits will be a major influence on the performance and life expectancy of your secondary cells. Unlike primary cells—in which the performance, particularly in terms of voltage, tends to decline steadily toward the end of the cell's service life—a nickel-cadmium battery maintains its voltage and current much longer in its life cycle and then suddenly drops dramatically in performance. This point is called the *operating ledge*. You can actually control where it will come to a significant degree—from after as little as ten minutes of use of your computer to several hours at the keyboard.

1. Efficient battery management and maintenance start from the moment you unpack the computer. You have the opportunity to condition the nicad to give its best performance. The normal procedure is that you must charge the battery fully before you use the computer for the first time. With many models this may take between eight and twelve hours, while others have fast-charging systems that reduce the time. Because the technology is advancing so rapidly, always check the owner's manual for appropriate procedure. It really does pay to get the full story on battery maintenance before you start using your hardware and not, as with other aspects of hardware and software, switch it on and try to make things work, only referring to the manual as a last resort.

2. Try to achieve a complete discharge and recharge cycle at least three times to give your battery a memory of the way it is supposed to behave. If you only half discharge it before recharging, it will memorize that pattern as what is expected and will behave accordingly.

Complete discharge means going well beyond the point at which the low-power light starts to flash. Computer manufacturers tend to be over-cautious about warning you when you are running out of electrical power, just as auto manufacturers give an early warning of a low gasoline level in the tank. So the low-power light will probably come on just as you reach that operating ledge. You should still have several minutes left to save your current work to disk or to plug in the mains adapter.

3. Develop a habit of immediately saving what you are doing as soon as the low-power light starts flashing. On computers that have an unreliable low-power indication, or with visual and/or audible warnings that are easily missed, it can be worthwhile saving to a different file name. If the battery power goes below the operating level during a long save, you risk saving garbage.

If this happens while you are overwriting the original file, you may lose that data, also. When operating portables on battery power, pay particular attention to saving data and don't be caught working on a long file that has not been saved for some time, or trying to save to the original file when battery power is borderline. You risk destroying what was saved earlier as well as losing your current work.

4. The battery-conditioning procedure should be followed when the computer is being used for the first time or when reconditioning an existing battery that has acquired bad habits. Leave the computer on after you have safely saved your current work. The battery will continue to discharge to the point where the disk drives will not run or the backlight will not come on. The characters on the screen will become garbled and then disappear, and the low-power light will go out. Be very careful about reading or writing to disk during this time, in case erratic computer behavior damages your stored data or programming. Some computers have electronic safeguards against this, but don't depend on it.

5. After quite a short period of normal use, in which you will probably recharge your battery in a random way such as giving it a boost before taking a trip, the battery's memory will change to shorter periods of discharge and the operating ledge will be reached sooner. You may suddenly find that you get only a few minutes of battery life, especially if you are accessing the disks a great deal or have the backlight turned up. Then you will have to go through the conditioning process again, perhaps a number of times, before a new memory pattern is established.

6. The deep discharge necessary to condition a nicad battery can be achieved quickly and conveniently by special software programs, such as Traveling Software's Battery Watch or the utilities available as shareware

on laptop users' bulletin boards (see Figure 9-3). Battery Watch takes much of the uncertainty out of knowing whether the flashing low-power light is giving you three minutes or thirty seconds of warning. The interval varies because different computing activities consume different amounts of power.

Figure 9-3. Traveling Software's Battery Watch.

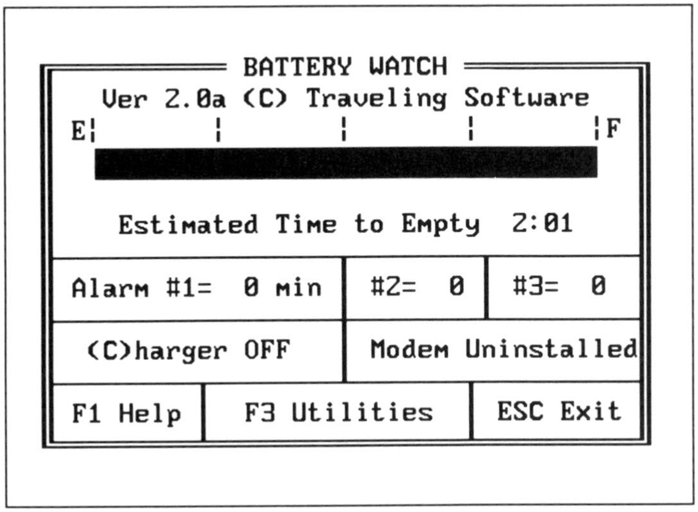

```
============ BATTERY WATCH ============
       Ver 2.0a (C) Traveling Software
   E|          |           |          |F
   ████████████████████████████████

        Estimated Time to Empty  2:01
   ┌─────────────────┬──────────┬──────────┐
   │ Alarm #1=  0 min │ #2=   0  │ #3=   0  │
   ├─────────────────┼──────────┴──────────┤
   │ (C)harger OFF    │ Modem Uninstalled   │
   ├───────────┬──────┴──────────┬──────────┤
   │ F1 Help   │ F3 Utilities    │ ESC Exit │
   └───────────┴─────────────────┴──────────┘
```

Battery Watch monitors how you are using your computer and what power is being drawn by the disks, the screen, and other components. It keeps regularly updating its predictions of how much battery power you have left. This can be called up at any time in the form of an on-screen display that functions very much like the gas gauge on your car.

The nicads can be seriously damaged—or even destroyed, with risk of damage to the computer also—if they are seriously overcharged. Normally there is a protection circuit that prevents overcharging if you operate the computer from the mains electrical supply through the adapter, but remember to physically disconnect the charger-adapter when you switch off the computer. If you are not going to need battery power for some time, it may be worth taking the battery pack out completely and just running from the mains adapter.

If you have persistently short battery life after trying to recondition with at least three full discharge and charge cycles, then one of the battery-pack cells may be defective. A quick and easy check is to put a voltameter across the battery after it has been charged fully to see if you get the voltage listed for your machine's specification. Normally a 12-volt battery pack should push out over 13 volts when fully charged and without a load.

If your computer has problems booting up from a fully charged battery but will do so when connected to an electrical outlet, it could be a symptom of a faulty battery. The voltage required for booting up is usually quite high as the disks spin and automatic diagnostic checks are made and programs loaded. If a fully charged battery cannot perform these tasks, it probably has a defect.

Lead-Acid Batteries

In the mid-1980s it would have seemed extraordinary to consider a future in portable computing for the ancient lead-acid battery technology. But the truth is that these tough, heavy electrical storage devices still account for over half of all the rechargeable batteries sold around the world. Recent technological developments have increased their potential for portable computing applications, as demonstrated in the Macintosh portables.

The traditional lead-acid battery in our automobiles that blew off inflammable gas and needed regular topping up with water has been replaced by sealed maintenance-free types. Now the corrosive liquid electrolyte acid can be formed into a gel to reduce the risk of spillage. So sealed-lead cells may well have a place in your computing present or future.

The Macintosh Portable has a very advanced lead-acid battery linked to a Mitsubishi 5073 power-management processor. This combination gives usable battery life of ten hours or more because the controller automatically switches off any components that are not being used. The whole machine goes into a sleep mode if it does not receive a keyboard or mouse instruction within periods that the user can vary from one to thirty minutes.

How to Conserve Power

Just as with a car, you can be extravagant with energy or conserve it carefully according to your "driving habits." Here are some tips for battery-power conservation.

- Having the backlight on at the lowest comfortable level will save a significant amount of battery power, as will limiting how often you access the disks. There are software programs and fine-tuning program tweaks that can reduce the amount of disk use, such as using DOS to create a RAM-drive device. Some of these were described in Chapter 3 in the section on software.

- Some computers are economical to run; others are the equivalent of gas guzzlers. If battery life is important to you, investigate how your prospective computer purchase manages battery power. At the very least you will want one that switches off the screen backlighting after a reasonably short period of inactivity. The more sophisticated systems have elaborate power-management capabilities that can double or triple battery life.

- Watch out particularly for power-wasting features such as internal modems that keep steadily draining energy from your batteries whether you use them or not. A self-powered external modem, or other peripherals that reduce the energy requirements of the computer itself, can increase your operating time substantially.

Electrical Adapters

An advantage with portables when plugged into electrical outlets is that their adapters usually compensate for the computing problems associated with "dirty" power. Desktop systems can malfunction and data be lost because of variations in voltage, caused by such problems as brownouts. These may occur frequently in some places during times of exceptional loads on the electrical supply, causing a drop in voltage. This can happen particularly during a heat wave, when there is an abnormal demand for power for air-conditioning units.

Voltage variations are not confined to the public electricity supply. They may occur on local circuits within a house or office when an appliance with a heavy current draw, such as a freezer, washing machine, or air-conditioning unit, starts up. In work situations, industrial power tools and welders are among the electrical equipment that can cause drops and surges in voltage. These variations can seriously damage a mains-powered computer system nearby, but against which the portable's adapter may offer some protection. Running a portable on its own batteries may be the safest and most cost-effective way of computing when power surges are a serious risk.

The adapter helps stabilize the incoming voltage—and perhaps also insulates a DC computer from variations in the AC cycles from a gas- or diesel-powered generator. Most adapters now feature automatic line selection, so that they adjust automatically to the voltage of the incoming power, needing no user action if you go from the United States, with our 110-volt electricity, to most foreign countries, where voltage varies between 220 volts and 250 volts. In some less-developed countries, particularly in rural areas, the official voltage may be far different from what is actually delivered at the outlets, and these fluctuations can damage sensitive electronic equipment. Be careful of this if using a transportable or desktop working directly from a standard electrical supply.

Some adapters sold with portables in the United States have the Underwriters' Laboratory label, indicating that they will only operate on 110 or 120 volts and 60 Hz when, in fact, they contain circuitry enabling them to switch to foreign standards. Check with your supplier if you want to use your adapter overseas and it is not clearly labeled as suitable for such use.

You can also convert to other voltages when overseas by plugging the adapter into a transformer, but be careful to use the right type. Most of the cheap voltage converters sold in luggage departments and drugstores are not suitable for use with most computers or other sensitive electronic equipment. They convert 240 volts to 110 volts by rapidly interrupting the current. Their output is not sufficiently pure, and they may not be able to cope with the peak power draw. You need a true transformer, which is heavier and more expensive, but able to deliver pure power.

The foreign traveler's adapter sets are suitable for enabling the plug on your adapter to fit into outlets that differ from U.S. standards. One potential problem is that most of these are designed for lightweight travel appliances and so are not grounded. If your adapter has a three-prong plug—the large prong being the ground connection—you need to use a special grounding adapter to make it compatible with foreign outlets.

In addition to reducing voltage to the level that your computer requires, the electrical adapter includes a DC rectifier that converts alternating current to direct current, usually at between 12 and 18 volts DC.

Always use the adapter supplied with your computer and do not be tempted to hook up another, even if it has the same input and output ratings, without expert advice. One day we may achieve standardization so that we need to carry only one adapter to power everything—computer, printer, portable copier, and other accessories—but it has not happened yet.

If you have to use another adapter not specified or approved by the manufacturer of your hardware, perhaps in an emergency, ensure that its output matches up and that it is of the correct polarity. Usually the center of the male plug that goes into the computer is negative and the outer contact is positive, but there are variations. The polarity should be marked on the outside of the adapter, but that's no help if you don't have it with you! In that situation, you need an electrical meter, or you may be able to check polarity by connecting a battery tester across the contacts on the adapter's output.

With most portables you can leave the adapter plugged in all the time you are using the computer, but you will need to remove it if the computer is switched off. Usually the battery automatically remains on charge while the adapter is connected, so there is the risk of overcharging.

The earlier and cheaper portables tend to take six to eight hours to recharge a flat battery. If you have upgraded, you may need to change your battery-management habits if your new machine has a fast-charge capability. This capability gets your battery up to full strength in an hour or two. Usually, when the computer is being operated the battery is being trickle-charged at a low rate at the same time, and there is no risk of overdoing things.

Check your manual for the correct way to plug in the adapter. Get it wrong—especially in a panic when the low-power light starts flashing—and you may lose your data. The usual procedure is to plug into the power source first—the outlet on the wall—and then put the adapter's output plug into the computer's input jack. Do it the other way round, and you will probably interrupt the power from the battery to the system and it will shut down—in the process eliminating any work you have not saved and possibly scrambling files if the power interruption occurs while you are reading or writing to disk.

Figure 9-4 shows the adapters supplied by Zenith for its popular Z-180 laptops. The figure also shows the correct procedure for plugging in.

Conventional Lead-Acid Batteries

Conventional lead-acid batteries can play an important role in many types of portable computing. Unlike the sealed lead-acid battery that's used in the Macintosh Portable, the conventional lead-acid battery has cells that are flooded with electrolyte, and so it must be kept upright. The battery will vent flammable gases if it is overcharged. Water must be added to maintain the electrolyte level, unless the battery is "maintenance-free," which means it has more than normal electrolyte and special venting to control evaporation.

There is a battery like this in your car, truck, recreational vehicle, or boat; most portables hook up to it via the cigarette lighter socket. If your computer uses the standard automotive 12-volt DC power, then the

Figure 9-4.   Adapters from Zenith for its Z-180 laptops.

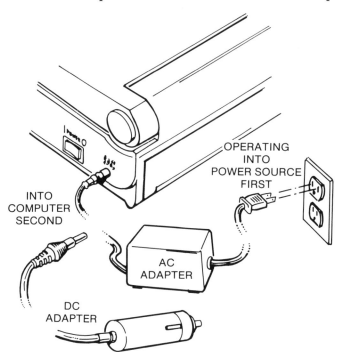

connection is easy. It requires only an adapter in the form of a power cord, with a plug to go into the lighter socket at one end and another plug to fit into the computer's socket at the other end. This should be available as an accessory from your computer supplier, or can be purchased at electronics and automotive equipment stores. However, if you are buying a DC adapter not specially designed to work with your computer, make sure the output is of the correct polarity or you risk damaging the computer.

Another potential for damage is starting the vehicle while the computer is plugged in. The starter draws so much power that the resulting sudden and extreme change in current flowing through the vehicle's electrical system can cause a surge that will damage the computer. These surges are easily observed if you start your car with the headlights on. The lights first dim, then brighten.

A vehicle's cigarette lighter socket is one of the most readily available alternative power sources for a portable computer when there is no 110- or 220-volt electrical outlet around. It can be used both to recharge the computer's own battery or for direct operation. The computer can be powered well away from the vehicle by using an extension cord, another automotive-supply-store item costing between about $10 and $15. However-er, some of these extension cords are not particularly well made, so check that it will handle current required by your system. Also, be sure it is connected properly so that the polarity at the outlet is not reversed. Some extensions have the positive and negative leads marked, or you can check with a meter.

If your computer requires a DC input other than 12 volts, you will need to use a converter when running it from a car battery. If possible, use one recommended or supplied by the computer's manufacturer. Do not be tempted to get any of those plug-in converters sold in automotive and electronics stores. Most do not have the capacity to cope with the current drawn by laptops. For the typical laptop you will need a heavy-duty converter, most readily available from specialty electronics stores. In addition to ensuring that it meets your computer's requirements for voltage and current, double-check that the output polarity is compatible. Some of these converters come with a plug in the output lead that lets you reverse the polarity; some also include a selection of output plugs to fit a variety of sockets. When ringing the polarity and plug changes, always double-check that everything is correct before hooking up.

Lead-acid batteries can be used to make a desktop system transportable. There are a number of ways of achieving this. The most expensive is to use an uninterruptible power supply specially designed for computer systems. These are designed to provide backup power if the electrical supply fails. They typically cost several hundred dollars and provide only limited emergency operating time, perhaps only ten minutes—just enough for you to save current work to your hard disk.

More practical for portable applications are one or more lead-acid batteries driving the computer directly through a 12-volt DC power hookup, or supplying alternating current from an outlet through an inver-ter. The first option can be as simple as connecting to a car cigarette lighter accessory socket linked to the battery terminals with alligator clips, remembering to get the polarity correct. This may be adequate to power a laptop and its peripherals, such as a printer or modem, for extended periods in the field or in other situations in which connecting to the mains is impractical. An example would be a system mounted on a trolley moving around a warehouse, factory, or construction site.

You can get more power choices and the opportunity to use 110-volt desktop equipment by combining lead-acid batteries with an inverter. This takes the DC power from the battery—or battery bank, if several are hooked up together to increase capacity—and converts it to AC power. Inverters used to pose all kinds of problems, particularly because their operating efficiency was so low they might deplete the battery faster than the appliances they were powering. In recent years they have been vastly improved, but you still pay for what you get. The cheapest ones are almost always either inefficient or barely powerful enough to run a computer, especially if you want to enjoy one of the advantages of this kind of portable setup and combine your laptop with a full-size mains monitor, which may draw 60 watts or more.

An indication of the potential for creative combinations of computer hardware with inverters and battery power is how Christopher Freitas, a design engineer with Photocomm, Inc., the specialist energy equipment suppliers, uses a new generation 100-watt inverter to run a Macintosh Plus with a hard disk and an Imagewriter printer from his car battery.

The computer system—a standard electrically powered setup—draws 5 amps. Christopher can do about four hours' computing with the standard 20 amp/hour car battery and still have enough power remaining to start the vehicle and recharge the battery from the car's alternator. Modern automotive alternators are very efficient and can restore a battery to full charge very quickly, so this kind of setup can be practical when computing away from an electrical outlet, enabling work to be continued with fewer interruptions than if you are dependent on recharging the computer's own internal batteries.

This inverter costs only about $150 and is good for extended use of laptops away from electrical outlets. It also enables static computing equipment to run off 12-volt DC batteries. Increasingly, portable computers are being used for extended periods in places where no electric supply is available, so limited battery life is a big problem. The African Wildlife Preservation Trust uses the same inverters to run laptops at its village outposts and in the off-road vehicles from which it carries out wildlife research in the most remote places. The computers are used so much that the vehicles are equipped with a supplementary battery primarily to recharge the batteries in the laptops.

To calculate what size inverter you need for your system, add up the wattage of all the equipment you will run at any one time: printer, computer, fax, telecommunications system, fan or air conditioner, lighting, and so on. Most equipment has the wattage on the label near the power lead, or you can calculate by multiplying the listed amperage by the voltage.

This will give you the continuous rating, but you will need to get an inverter that will cope also with the higher surge—or peak-power—rating, because appliances take a greater load at startup, or to perform specific functions. For example, a laptop AC adapter may be rated at only 20 watts of steady-state power, but 33 watts for peak-power capacity. A television set or monitor may have a surge rating double that of its continuous rating, while an air conditioner needs a surge capacity three or four times that of its power requirements when running steadily.

Add up the continuous-rating requirements and the surge ratings for your proposed system to produce two totals, both of which must be well within the capacity ratings for the inverter. Combine the inverter with one or more batteries, and you can have electrical power available virtually anywhere.

You can build up battery banks that are tailored to your portable computer and other power needs. By connecting batteries in parallel—the positive terminals linked to each other and the negative terminals coupled together—the voltage remains the same as for the individual batteries, but you increase the capacity of the battery bank to deliver power over a long period.

There are special industrial batteries of 2 and 6 volts. They can be linked to a solar panel or generator in series and parallel configurations to combine the desired voltage with increased capacity.

The lead-acid batteries used in such power-storage systems should be of the deep-cycle type, which are different from conventional car batteries. The difference is similar to that between a sprinter and a long-distance runner. The car battery is designed to give out a lot of energy for a short time before it hands over to the alternator the prime responsibility for supplying the car's electrical needs. The deep-cycle battery steadily provides electrical energy over a long period. It will also stand repeated deep discharges and recharging, while a car battery will rapidly deteriorate under such operating conditions.

Generators, the Sun, and the Wind

Immediate, portable power at any time is obtainable from gas or diesel generators that have been greatly improved in recent years to be more reliable, efficient, and quieter. Using a generator to recharge your battery bank may enable you to keep the size of the bank very small.

However, in many applications, using the natural energy of the sun or the wind may be a more attractive approach. Particularly impressive developments have been made recently in the field of solar energy, so that solar panels can, when linked to storage batteries, provide a complete portable power system.

Photocomm and other specialists in this field provide boxed kits that fit most applications and are easy to hook up. You can find them in good recreational vehicle and marine stores. There are configurations covering a mobile office with a laptop, printer, and other equipment that could be installed in a van or RV. Higher-capacity systems that are either mobile or located away from standard electrical supplies are capable of driving desktop computers and peripherals through an inverter.

Microprocessors

The Mac Portable and other recent portable computers demonstrate how power-miserly microprocessors can extend battery life. That is an option worth considering to improve the battery performance of existing machines.

Replacement chips are becoming available that use only one-third of the power of their predecessors; Intel's 80C287A math coprocessor is an example. Unfortunately, upgrading portables is usually nowhere near as easy as it is to slip new chips and boards into desktop machines. Portables have tightly packed electronics, and, to increase reliability, many have their chips soldered into place, making them difficult to remove.

10

Bringing It All Together

However much hardware or software you have assembled, it does not constitute a computerized information system until everything is brought together into a functioning whole that can carry out tasks.

This may be a complex undertaking, even when using portables. It is even more complicated when portables have to be integrated into a corporate information system that may already have desktops, minis, and mainframes. If the whole system is not planned properly, the portables cannot meet their full potential to increase personal productivity, let alone properly benefit the organization as a whole.

Alan Freedman, in his excellent book *The Computer Glossary* (New York: AMACOM, 1989) and in his lectures, uses the diagram shown in Figure 10-1 to represent how the elements of any hardware and software combination relate to each other to create the information system that generates the database, that in turn becomes the processed information in the management system required to devise the strategies, tactics, plans, and controls to achieve an organization's goals. Freedman describes a complex methodology to develop such a system, but a less complex, and still methodical approach will pay off even when you are building a simple portable system for your own personal use. You may not need all the expert input from other people, but you should still go through the phases of defining your information requirements, putting together the software and hardware combination that will satisfy those needs, and then making sure that the system as a whole works in the most efficient way.

Figure 10-1. How the elements of any hardware and software combination relate.

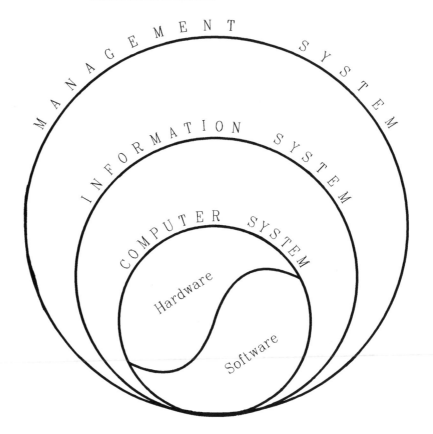

Do this right and portable computers will be an enormous benefit to personal and corporate productivity. Indeed, portable systems with their stand-alone flexibility can help demonstrate that some data processing networks no longer make sense, especially if they were created so workers could share equipment, such as laser printers and hard disks, which have become comparatively inexpensive. Also, bulletin boards accessible to portable systems away from base as well as desktops can be much more cost-effective for electronic mail than a network.

There is an important factor to consider when building a portable system: It should be able to function in two environments. The portable system could well be two distinct but related systems—one when it is at home or in the office (the *base* mode) and the other when it is on the road (the *mobile* mode).

Portables at Home

Whether your portable is your only computer or an addition to an existing system, it needs a comfortable home. Its use will be greatly extended if you set it up in some kind of docking facility so that it hooks up easily to such peripherals as another computer, to a network with which you need to exchange data, or to a printer, modem, and other accessories.

Some portables are built to this principle, like the Compaq SLT/286 with its sophisticated optional desktop expansion base providing facilities such as networking connections and battery charging. In this way, the portable makes a smooth transition from the base to the mobile mode.

The exploded view of the Compaq LTE (Figure 10-2) shows how desktop computing power is being packed into modern portables. The trend is toward modular construction and to find new ways of shrinking or eliminating the bulkier and heavier mechanical components, notably the fixed and floppy disk drives.

A similar approach is seen in the GRiDCase 1535 EXP, which has two XT/A expansion slots in a tray easy to snap on or off.

But you still have to connect a variety of terminals to complete the hardware side of a system.

The base and working area should be near a power source and telephone, if possible. There should be a level, secure surface for both the computer and its peripherals. Most manufacturers recommend an environmental range of between 10 and 40 degrees Centigrade, with 20 to 80 percent relative humidity.

The system should not be in direct sunlight, and dust and other airborne contaminants should be minimized as much as possible. Under extreme conditions, I store my laptop in a strong, sealed plastic bag—one of the large Ziplocs designed for holding clothes or bulk freezer packs. I put in a fresh package of silica gel as well, to prevent moisture buildup.

Furniture for Portables

It can be worthwhile getting specific furniture to provide a functional base for the portable system. The compactness of portable computers and their peripherals enables them to fit very efficiently into or onto furniture that can make the whole system move as one mobile unit. One reason the portable scores here is that it makes vertical as well as horizontal configurations easier to achieve.

For example, AnthroCarts (see Figure 10-3) are part of a range of

(*text continues on page 150*)

Figure 10-2.   Compaq LTE/286 and Compaq LTE.

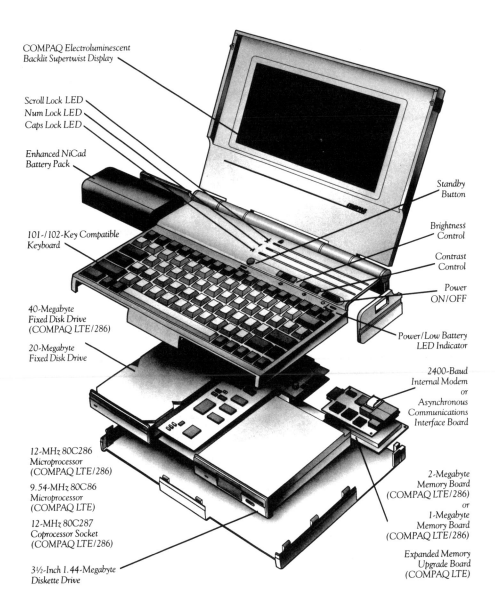

COMPAQ Electroluminescent
Backlit Supertwist Display

Scroll Lock LED
Num Lock LED
Caps Lock LED

Enhanced NiCad
Battery Pack

101-/102-Key Compatible
Keyboard

40-Megabyte
Fixed Disk Drive
(COMPAQ LTE/286)

20-Megabyte
Fixed Disk Drive

12-MHz 80C286
Microprocessor
(COMPAQ LTE/286)

9.54-MHz 80C86
Microprocessor
(COMPAQ LTE)

12-MHz 80C287
Coprocessor Socket
(COMPAQ LTE/286)

3½-Inch 1.44-Megabyte
Diskette Drive

Standby
Button

Brightness
Control

Contrast
Control

Power
ON/OFF

Power/Low Battery
LED Indicator

2400-Baud
Internal Modem
or
Asynchronous
Communications
Interface Board

2-Megabyte
Memory Board
(COMPAQ LTE/286)
or
1-Megabyte
Memory Board
(COMPAQ LTE/286)

Expanded Memory
Upgrade Board
(COMPAQ LTE)

units that can be customized in dozens of ways as stand-alones or in combination with static furniture.

The Portland, Oregon, manufacturer carries out a great deal of research in furniture technology. Following is a checklist of base-station factors, drawing on the recommendations of its experts and the experiences of myself and other portable computer users. Many of these points will influence how you put your system together to take it on the road.

1. Identify the users: Find out who is actually using the portable computers in your organization. The needs and wants of a vice-president may be very different from those of a secretary, a reporter, a salesman, or an engineer.

2. Look at the application: Identify and list how and where the

Figure 10-3. AnthroCarts.

portable computers are being used. Take particular note of the following factors:

- *Can you accommodate all the hardware?* Consider the computer itself, the monitor, the keyboard and mouse, the printer, the modem, the separate disk drives if there are any, the power supply, and additional peripherals.
- *What is the flow of work and activity between the user and the hardware?* What items are used the most—and what the least? What needs to be positioned in front of the user, or at the side?
- *How much space is available?* Is it better to spread out vertically or horizontally?
- *Where is the system being used?* Are there any special environmental considerations; for example, a clean room, an industrial location, or an office?
- *Does the system as a whole have to be moved around, or just the portable components detached and taken elsewhere?* Is it better to have mobile or stationary furniture? If mobile, what kind of surface will it roll over—thick carpets, rough concrete? Will it need to go into elevators or vehicles?
- *Does the user need to change cables at the back of the computer frequently or have other particular access needs?*
- *Would it be better to exploit the flexibility of a portable and make this a stand-up application?* Or should this be one in which the position of the user can be varied for comfort, health, and convenience?

3. List the requirements for the ideal furniture to provide a base for your system.

- *Flexibility, durability, and stability.* Ensure that it is adaptable to future needs and will safely hold the thousands of dollars' worth of hardware in the system—both while you are working and when moving from place to place. Pay particular attention to the quality of the castors and their suitability for carpets or rough surfaces.
- *Modularity.* It should adjust to fit both the hardware it contains and the people using it.
- *Footprint.* The base should fit into the minimum space available.
- *Cord management.* Even battery-powered portables can generate a

cat's cradle of umbilical cables. Good furniture will have facilities for keeping these cords under control.

- *Printed paper flow*. The paper must flow smoothly from the stack into the printer and out again, whether it is continuous stationery or single sheets. The user must be able to get to the printer to check what is going on and to change or add paper.

- *Access*. The user must be able to get easily to connections, switches, and controls of both the computer and the peripherals, especially when portable components have to be removed or reconnected before and after trips.

- *Comfort and screen glare*. As soon as you hook it up to anything else, your portable loses much of its mobility, including the ease with which you can change your work position. A problem is positioning the screen so that it can be seen clearly. Fluorescent lights can pose particular difficulties. The furniture must either adjust or be mobile enough to meet these comfort and efficiency requirements.

- *Aesthetics*. The furniture should look good as well as function efficiently.

Creative Options

The enormous range of situations in which portable systems are used stimulates creative setups. The portable is ideal to create a standing workstation, or one that can be moved easily between standing or sitting positions or from place to place. Standing up at a computer and frequently changing position can help avoid health problems such as carpal tunnel syndrome (see Appendix B).

For example, there is a folding Barn Desk made of steel that can be hung on a kitchen, factory, or warehouse wall just as readily as in a cow shed to note milking schedules. It has two main components: the back with predrilled holes from which to hang it and a base flap that hinges down and is suspended by chains in the working position. The cost is between $35 and $55 depending on finish.

There are obvious variations on this theme in wood or metal, available pre-made or built to order. One of the cleverest devices commercially available to provide a secure, firm surface for a portable computer anywhere is the Laptop Workstation from Curtis Manufacturing, a Rolodex subsidiary (Figure 10-4).

You can put the Workstation on a desk, table, or even your lap, and it will hold any size laptop securely, in a choice of tilted positions. There are secure containers for diskettes on one side and space on the other for a mouse and pad, a portable printer, or an adjustable, built-in copy stand. The elements can be changed around for left-handed users. The whole workstation folds up to slip into a bag or briefcase and sells for under $80.

Portables on the Road

The secret to building the fully mobile side of your portable system is, like packing for any business trip, knowing what to leave behind. Now that pocket organizers are so sophisticated and can exchange data with bulkier portables and desktops, you may prefer two separate but coordinated work-to-go systems.

Figure 10-4.   The Laptop Workstation from Curtis Manufacturing.

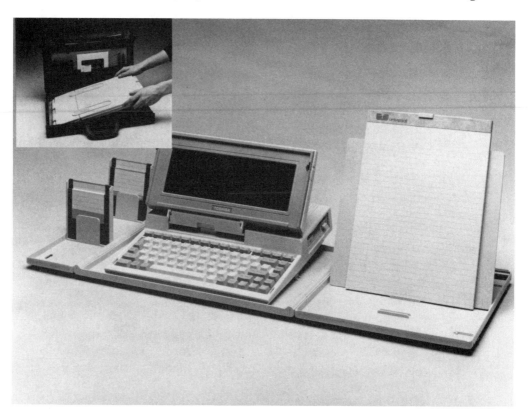

One might be based on your pocket notebook or organizer for those trips where they are able to provide all the personal information management needs that you have, plus their limited database and number processing abilities.

The second system is more comprehensive in line with a portable office for situations when you need greater capacity.

In either case, the worst way to construct the portable system is hastily putting together for each trip what you think you will need from the scattered components, disks, and other elements lying around. At the very least have a travel checklist to make sure nothing gets left behind. Figure 10-5 is a useful checklist.

Let's go through the list in detail, mainly to see what you can leave out.

1. *The computer and/or pocket organizer.* This obviously cannot be left behind because it is the nucleus of the system. But you may have more choice than you at first think. Consider the size, weight, and sophistication required in work-to-go situations. Try not to duplicate your desktop resources unnecessarily.

Make sure the batteries are charged so that the computer is ready to be used; you may be asked to demonstrate it as you go through security checks at the airport, to prove it doesn't contain a bomb. Follow the manufacturer's instructions for parking the hard disk heads and placing disks or protectors in the floppy drive slots.

2. *Applications programs.* These should all have been transferred to working disks, or copied to your hard disk, or both. Obviously you do not take the originals away from a safe base and subject them to the risks of travel. It can be worthwhile write-protecting the applications programs by moving the tabs on microfloppies, if they will work in this mode. You may never get your disks mixed up on your desk, but you can easily do so under adverse conditions on the road.

Pack all disks well away from stray magnetic fields that might be generated by other equipment, such as transformers. For additional protection from magnetism and X-rays, put your disks into the lead-lined bags used to protect photographic film when traveling.

3. *Data disks.* Take however many formatted blank disks you think you may need, plus copies of existing data files that you might require. Using different colors of actual disks or of labels can help identify different files and applications more easily.

4. *Additonal backup and blank disks.* Microfloppies are available

Figure 10-5.   Checklist for packing your portable system.

	TRAVEL CHECKLIST	Serial #
1	Computer and/or pocket organizer	
2	Applications programs	
3	Data disks	
4	Additional backup and blank disks	
5	Transformer and/or adapter	
6	Spare batteries	
7	Extension cord, surge protector, plug adapters	
8	Printer	
9	Printer adapter	
10	Paper and spare ink cartridge or ribbon	
11	Printer cable	
12	Spare printer batteries and/or recharger	
13	Modem	
14	Modem spare battery and/or adapter	
15	Modem cables and telephone hookup kit	
16	Portable fax	
17	Fax transformer or adapter	
18	Scanner and cables	
19	Documentation	
20	Customs form completed for all equipment	
21	Pocket memo and tapes, calculator, agenda, business cards, pens and pencils, and other small items	

almost everywhere the business traveler goes. But even in big cities, the law that decrees that toast always hits the carpet butter side down also ensures that you will need disks only when the stores are closed. When going to remote areas or overseas—where the type you want may be difficult or impossible to obtain, and probably more expensive if you can find it—take half again as many disks as you think you may need.

5. *Transformer and/or adapter.* What a bore these are: heavy, ugly things with tangled wires leading in and out. The buttered-toast law ensures that if you leave it behind, you are bound to need your adapter. At least put it in your checked baggage if you can be sure you will not need it during the journey. You might be able to put together a system so that the computer, printer, and peripherals run off the same adapter, but be warned that a warranty almost certainly will be invalidated if you use an adapter not authorized by the manufacturer.

The notebook and pocket computers or organizers get long battery life from disposable cells and can eliminate the need for adapters, which is a strong factor in their favor.

6. *Spare batteries.* Although disposable batteries are more readily available than spare disks, batteries often run down at the most inconvenient time, so a spare set is essential. I wrap the separate cells in a bundle held together with a rubber band, and these go in Ziploc plastic sandwich bags stuffed into my shoes. That way they travel well protected and cannot short-circuit. (My transformers usually go in my shoes also, but I've got big feet so that may not be a packing option for you.)

7. *Extension cord, surge protector, transformer, plug adapters.* The only one of these items I always carry in the United States is the plug adapter, a small rubberized device that converts two-pin outlets to take three-pin plugs. If you are staying in a major hotel, you can nearly always hook up to a reasonably stable electrical outlet close enough to where you want to work. The transformer and plug adapters are necessary for international travel, although most of the voltage adapters supplied with portable computing equipment sold in the United States will work on 110 or 220-240 volts.

8. *Printer.* Leave it behind if you can do without it or can use one at your destination. Then you can leave the next three items out of your baggage as well. I have yet to need to use a printer in an airport or on a flight, so my printer always goes in checked baggage. Unfortunately, there is no printer made yet that will fit in even my large shoes, so it needs careful packing.

9. *Printer adapter*. Unfortunately, the computer and portable printer manufacturers have not got together yet to standardize their adapters, so you have to take one of each with you. Some portables, like the perennially popular Kodak Diconix, will run on disposable cells, which eliminates the adapter-charger if there is sufficient battery power for your needs.

10. *Paper and spare ink cartridge or ribbon*. These are more checked-baggage items that you will probably need when they are not readily obtainable and when the paper supplied by your hotel does not give good results.

11. *Printer cable*. The computer will not drive the printer without it, and a cable is well worth packing even if you do not take the printer, because you may need to hook up to another printer at your destination. You can get cables that are flat and bend more easily than the stiff, bulky, and heavy desktop variety. I always pack my cables along with my spare trouser belt around the perimeter at the bottom of my suitcase, held in a loop with rubber bands.

12. *Spare printer batteries and/or recharger*. See item 6 above, although another option with some printers is to take rechargeable cells and a separate charger unit, especially if the same cells will fit another item in your baggage, such as a flashlight, radio, or shaver.

13. *Modem*. If you do not have one built into your computer, select a modem for your portable that is light and strong so it will pack inside shoes of any size to travel securely as checked baggage. Some of the best modem deals have been part of joining-up packages offered by Prodigy and other on-line services.

14. *Modem spare battery and/or adapter*. Eliminate these if you can. There are small modems that plug straight into an electrical outlet or run off the computer's power supply. And how often do you really need to use a modem when there is not an electrical outlet near the telephone?

15. *Modem cables and telephone hookup kit*. These items are covered in Chapter 8. The screwdriver and tweezers or pliers should be the only computing tools you actually need on the road. If you are not going equipped for telecommunications, then pack a small screwdriver separately. At one time Zenith was giving away a neat standard and Phillips head pocket screwdriver as a promotion at shows.

16. *Portable fax*. Only include this if you must and your facsimile-transmission needs cannot be met by the computer and modem, or the hotel or other public fax services now readily available.

17. *Fax transformer or adapter*. Perhaps your printer or other electronic equipment can provide an electrical adapter or battery power of the correct voltage or polarity. You should be able to do your fax transmission and receiving at times when these peripherals are not needed, and so can borrow their power supplies.

18. *Scanner*. Not part of most portable systems, but they can be very useful on the road. Having one with you might eliminate the need for a separate fax or portable copying machine, while a scanner and a portable computer make a much underutilized tool for collecting research material in libraries and other reference places. The hand-held scanners need not take up much space in your baggage, but they do need secure packing. (Do not forget any cables or software that your scanner might need.)

19. *Documentation*. Bulky manuals are a nuisance on the road, but you can use hard-copy quick references for the main features, select programs with good help facilities, take along tutorial disks, or create your own crib sheets on disk. If you have written special macros to automate often-needed functions, print out a list of these and stow it with your traveling equipment. Taking along a record of technical support help lines can be a lifesaver; write the numbers on the appropriate disks, in your address book or on labels stuck to the equipment.

Essential documentation is your name and telephone number on every item of equipment in case something gets lost. Some people tape their business cards to the bottom or side of each piece. You can even include your name, address, telephone number, and an offer of reward to the end of the autoexec.bat file on the hard disk or on self-booting floppy disks. That way the screen will display a message identifying you as the owner.

On long trips at home or overseas, it can be worth taking evidence of purchase and warranty in case you need these.

20. *Customs form completed for all equipment*. You require this if you travel overseas. You get the list accredited by a U.S. Customs official before you leave, and then produce it on your return to show that you are bringing into the country goods for which the duties and taxes have already been paid.

You can make the list up once, create several copies, and then strike off the copied list before it is stamped anything not on a particular trip.

21. *Travel checklist*. The list itself helps to keep everything together and organized during a trip. I suggest you either copy the list and refer to it before each trip, or customize it to your needs and then copy it.

Leave one copy of the list at home and take two copies with you—one in your carry-on and the other in your checked luggage. These can be invaluable if luggage is lost or delayed, or if you need to report a theft and make an insurance claim.

How Do You Carry It All?

The carrying case for your portable system is at least as important as the furniture that houses it back at base.

Soft Cases. You need to look for a tough outer covering that will repel water. Coated nylon is among the best materials. Leather looks good, but makes for a heavier case that will scuff more easily.

There should be adequate padding between the outer covering and the inner lining, the latter being of a material such as brushed nylon that will not scratch your equipment, yet will stand up to considerable rubbing.

Avoid metal zippers and fastenings. Molded nylon hardware is strong, less likely to scratch you or your computer, and will not corrode. All zippers should be self-healing. It is very useful to have pockets and internal compartments with movable spacers that fasten and unfasten easily and can have their dimensions varied because they use Velcro or similar hook-and-loop fabric fastenings. The quality of the webbing, reinforcement points, and stitching should be examined closely.

The main features of a quality Pace case are shown in Figure 10-6.

This laptop tote pack is one of the easiest ways of carrying a full-size portable on a plane or in other difficult situations. The computer can be left

Figure 10-6. The main features of a quality Pace case.

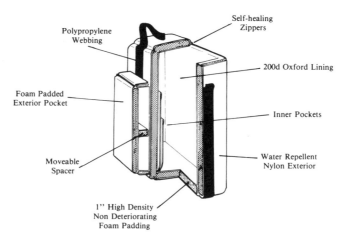

in the case, or removed easily whether the case is horizontal or vertical.

The outer pocket is padded also, to protect a printer or other ancillary equipment. This case, and some others, can convert to a backpack—ergonomically by far the best way of carrying a heavy load over any distance, although not very convenient in airports or in aircraft, when bags tend to be put down and lifted up at frequent intervals.

Many laptops—and certainly all notebook computers—will go into a standard briefcase. Particularly practical are soft-sided cases, but make sure they are of good quality, so that zippers, handles, and stitching accommodate the stresses of heavy electronic equipment, plus papers and other odds and ends. Internal pockets and adjustable padded shoulder straps are important features also.

Some systems have customized cases to make them as convenient and functional as possible. GRiD System's portable cellular workstation holds the laptop and a cellular phone in the same case and can be put into action by just unzipping sections.

Peripheral equipment and accessories can travel better in custom cases. The 12-volt portable battery pack from Product Corporation (see Figure 10-7) comes in a compact case, smart enough for any occasion and for easy connection to power the laptop for extended use away from AC power supplies.

Figure 10-7. A 12-volt portable battery pack.

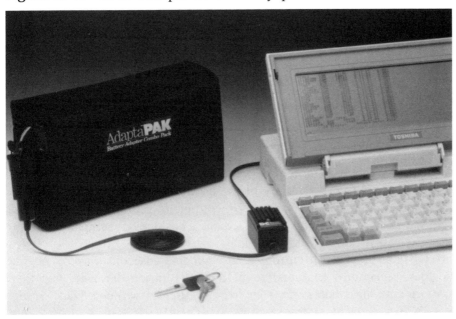

Figure 10-8. A boxier case for a lunchbox portable.

The lunchbox portable needs a boxier case (see Figure 10-8). Pace has evolved a special clam design for easy access and added pockets for such items as printer or cables. These bags can also be practical for smaller laptops with lots of ancillary equipment.

There are customized bags to carry the different Macintosh models and turn them into transportables. One very practical container for the SE models has a separate pocket for the keyboard, a comfortable mouse house in the lid, a lockable pocket for disks, and a foam spacer that enables something heavy and bulky, like an extra disk drive, to be carried without hitting against anything else (see Figure 10-9).

More basic versions are cheaper and put everything inside the main body of the case. There is also a custom case that holds the Imagewriter printer.

Hard Cases. The best protection for your system on the road is a hard-shell case. There is now a wide selection made of very light but immensely strong metal alloys that, quite frankly, have made heavy and less durable leather cases outmoded for carrying valuable, vulnerable electronic equipment.

There are a number of specialty suppliers listed in Appendix F, or you can extend the choice by looking at the vast variety of hard-shell photographic equipment cases. Many of these can be customized to hold your computer, printer, and other items by cutting, or removing precut cubes, from the foam interior until each piece has a customized compartment into which it will fit snugly.

Of course, you can customize any suitable case this way by buying the foam separately, trimming it to fit tightly inside the case, and then using a craft or other knife—one with a slightly serrated blade works best—to carve out the compartments. This is a great way to customize a

Figure 10-9. A customized bag for carrying a Macintosh and turning it into a transportable.

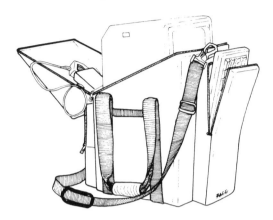

backpack. I used the same technique to create a really tough home for a complete system inside a gun case.

Always test a hard case to see if it will stand up properly. Some have rounded bottoms and tip over very easily, which means you have to prop them against a wall or, more often because there is no convenient wall nearby, against your legs as you line up to check in and board. That can become a real pain.

Carrying Tips. All cases should feel balanced when you carry them fully loaded. Some that look great in the store go all lopsided when the computer and printer are put in them.

Thin, floppy shoulder straps soon get twisted and are much more likely to get in a tangle on the ground, picking up dirt and water to transfer to your clothes and tripping yourself or fellow passengers.

Try to get your system on wheels if you can. Some of the hard cases have wheels built in, or you can customize good-quality wheeled luggage to accommodate computer gear. Soft cases can go onto collapsible luggage trolleys, but beware of the very cheap luggage carts that tend to collapse when you don't want them to.

If you fly frequently, be sure the portable system goes on and off the trolley easily. The case—with its own wheels or when on a trolley—should be narrow enough to trail behind you down the aisle of an aircraft without hitting the seats, and sufficiently stable not to fall over.

The idea is to lift your computer system out of the car or taxi and roll it all the way through to your seat on the aircraft. That way you avoid the back, shoulder, and neck problems that result from carrying heavy baggage.

If you need to carry your computer onto commercial flights, then the case must fit under a seat or in the overhead bin. The carry-on baggage limits are that it be no more than 9 × 14 × 22 inches to fit under the seat, or 4 × 32 × 45 inches for the overhead bin. You may be permitted something larger, but don't count on it.

There is greater flexibility and convenience with a soft case that will expand and contract to meet varying needs on the ground, when getting through the checkpoints into the plane, and when using your system in the air. However, durability, ease of access, and protection for your equipment are prime requirements. Do not forget that you may have to carry a load of thirty pounds or more for long distances through airports and this can be extremely hazardous to your health, especially if the bag is not designed well.

You can build mobile units easily in a van, recreational vehicle, or trailer, asking yourself the appropriate questions listed earlier for the base station. One of the most practical and low-cost ways of creating a computing unit on wheels is inside a pickup truck camper shell.

When Steven K. Roberts went *Computing Across America* (Medford, N.J.: Learned Information, Inc., 1988), he had several systems fixed to his bicycle, some that he could use while in motion and easily remove when he was working at stopovers. His book contains practical advice about bringing mobile systems together to meet very demanding circumstances.

Figure 10-10.   The ultimate lifestyle portable office.

I met the ultimate life-style portable office when I encountered jewelry designer Kate Drew-Wilkinson. She was taking advantage of a delightful spring day to move her monthly invoicing chores away from her desk and out into the open near San Francisco's Golden Gate Bridge (Figure 10-10).

Appendixes

Appendix A

Road Hazards: Theft, Accidents, Espionage, and Viruses

The business traveler's portable computer, like its owner, risks injury or infection while on the road. Most threatened are the promiscuous laptops that swap diskettes indiscriminately with strangers and don't care who they get intimate with on bulletin boards or at conferences and trade shows.

The virus risk adds a new dimension to the security problems inherent in traveling with a computer. The most serious of these are physical: your machine may be stolen or damaged. The consequences may go far beyond the actual loss of the hardware, which is probably covered by insurance. Valuable records may disappear also, especially if you have a hard disk and rely on that as your primary data storage.

Most insurance policies do not have adequate provision for lost data, if they cover this contingency at all. The most worthwhile insurance for your data costs no premiums and is just good computing practice. Back up all your work and keep the backup disks secure in a separate place from your system and current working records.

Physical Damage

Damage to your portable—by dropping or knocking it, for example—is the hazard most likely to temporarily deny you access to your data,

167

unless your computing habits make you an above-average virus risk. Although the hard disk and electronic components may need replacing if your portable gets a severe knock, it is probable that the disk reading and writing mechanism has slipped out of alignment and the data are still intact and can be recovered.

If you suspect the problem is a consequence of some physical stress on the computer, unless you really know what you are about, do not rush to use powerful utilities software that promises miracles in recovering lost data. Similarly, it is dangerous to delve into DOS for strong medicine unless you know the consequences of the commands you use.

Better, always, when valuable data are stored on a hard disk that is giving problems, is to consult an expert in data recovery, not a technician expert only in repairing or replacing disk drives. The firms that specialize in data recovery have a high success rate when given first access to a sick system. They blame most of their failures on the consequences of do-it-yourself surgery or intervention by technicians who destroy otherwise recoverable data while trying to fix the crashed disk.

You minimize your risks by always having backups readily available on removable disks—preferably two backup sets, with one to go on the road with you and the other safely stored at home or in the office. Obviously, you risk losing your backup disks if they are kept with your computer and it is stolen. Keep the backups separate. If your problems stem from a system malfunction, you always have the option of running your disks on another system while your hardware is being fixed.

Industrial Espionage

Data or other important confidential records can be compromised while traveling with your computer. Be particularly conscious of this when working in public places, such as airports. You may get used to curious fellow passengers glancing over your shoulder, but this annoying practice also poses a security risk if your work makes you a target for industrial espionage or a hacker hoping to pick up a password or some other information that could help him to break into a network.

Industrial espionage is far, far more prevalent than most of us realize, especially in these times when advance product information, research data, or intellectual property can have such high value to a competitor. Treat your disks, your computer with data stored on it, and the displays on your screen with at least as much caution as you would if they were confidential hard-copy documents.

Be particularly careful at trade conferences and other gatherings, where industrial espionage activities are most likely to take place. They may not be directed specifically at you, but might be in the form of a general sweep to find out what is going on in a particular industry or business sector. I spent nearly two years researching the theft by pirate copying of intellectual property and branded products. My files contain information about industrial espionage in all kinds of business activities, including computer companies where undercover agents traded cocaine for information about new products and sifted through the garbage for corporate secrets.

Most victims do not realize they are threatened until something serious happens. Even if you have adequate security in the office, your regular precautions may break down when you take work or data on the road to process in your portable computer.

Phone lines on which you are transferring data can be tapped. The proliferation of faxes poses special risks of information getting into the wrong hands. Both problems are compounded by the laxity in handling guests' messages and the frequent staff changes characteristic of many hotels. Agents seeking information can gain temporary employment, and so get direct access to guest baggage, fax traffic, phone messages, or correspondence to guests and conference attenders.

Disks left in an unsafe place can be copied and returned without anyone ever suspecting. Hard copies and other documentation left lying around or dumped into the garbage can be worth a lot of money to your competitors, particularly if your products or services are tempting for the industrial pirates, whose commercial fakery now rivals in scale the international illicit drug trade.

Viruses

I have deliberately not gone into detail about encryption, passwords, or other conventional security procedures as ways to protect your data, because they can be compromised. None are much, if any, good against the now-serious threat of virus infections.

Computer viruses are the most prevalent of the malicious programming widely disseminated in the computing community. These virus programs are written so that they seize any opportunity to spread from one system to another. They create clones of themselves to further this infection, and they can be programmed to do a wide range of harmful or annoying things, from playing tunes on your computer's loudspeaker to trashing everything on your hard disk.

The rapid increase in virus infections in 1989 and 1990 probably means—just by simple mathematical progression—that a portable computer system has a more than one-in-ten chance of being infected. Those who network, download programs from bulletin boards, run pirated software, and use their disks in other systems or allow others to use their computers may well be approaching even odds of becoming virus victims.

There are over 100 distinct viral strains circulating in the PC environment common to virtually all portables. These hostile programs are becoming more sophisticated in their ability to spread from system to system, hide within other programs, and reproduce themselves very rapidly. Statistically, the epidemic can only get worse, even if no hacker ever writes another virus.

Of course, new viruses are constantly appearing, and the old ones are being hacked into more virulent form to outwit the detection programs. Ironically, the new viruses that periodically grab the headlines and cause scares in the computing community are not the major risk at any given time. When a virus is still rare and at the early stage of its infection cycle, it does not pose as big a risk for the average computer user as does a virus program that has been reproducing and spreading over a long period—the way the Pakistani Brain or the Jerusalem Virus that have been around for years hit many corporate and college systems.

One way that viruses spread so quickly among business computers is through what one victim described as "the software marketing whores," many of whom are laptop enthusiasts. These are salespeople who flit from company to company, looking for any opportunity to run demonstration programs. The disks go from one system to another, picking up and spreading self-replicating codes.

We are told to practice safe sex to protect our health. In the same way, we should practice safe computing to protect our data. We have reached the point where salespeople should find themselves most unwelcome if they try to run their disks on the systems of a potential client. That will give a further boost to portable computers, although many companies and government agencies are so concerned about viruses that they will not allow either their own staff or visitors to bring disks or unauthorized portables onto their premises.

Symptoms and Prevention of an Infection

Among the main symptoms of virus infection are programs becoming slower to load, the size of infected programs increasing, strange error messages appearing on the screen, or unusual system activity such as disk drive lights coming on for no obvious reason. However, many viruses generate no symptoms to warn you of their presence before they start destroying or altering data.

If infection is suspected, the safest action is to switch off the system, isolate any disks to which the virus might have spread, and seek expert advice, or run an antiviral program like PRO-SCAN, which is ideal for portables because it is so easy to use and has a very clear display on LCD monitor screens.

Be very careful if renting computers, or using business or desktop publishing or quick-print centers that do not take stringent antiviral precautions. If running your own programs or data on strange systems, transfer them first to backup disks and destroy these when the task is completed. Do not bring them away with you and risk their being inadvertently loaded into your home or office system.

Do not take any diskette on the road without first creating a backup to leave behind in a safe place.

You can find out more on this increasingly important topic by sending a stamped, self-addressed envelope to the International Computer Virus Institute, 1257 Siskiyou Boulevard, Suite 179, Ashland, Oregon 97520; or the Computer Virus Industry Association, 4423 Cheeney Street, Santa Clara, California 95054. Both recommend using quality shareware antiviral programs that can be updated from well-protected bulletin boards. The viruses are being modified so frequently and new ones created at such a rate that antiviral software that cannot be updated gives very limited protection.

Appendix B

Portable Computers and Health Matters

A major computing and human resources management issue of the 1990s that could be more important than new data processing technology, breakthroughs in system design, or revolutionary software is the fast-growing awareness that working at a computer keyboard can be hazardous to your health.

Indeed, the most common occupational injuries and diseases in the coming years will be computer-related problems such as repetitive stress injury; carpal tunnel syndrome; tendinitis; head, neck, and lower back pain and restricted movement; stress-related disorders; and eye dysfunction.

The good news for laptop users is that their equipment, unlike desktop systems, offers readily applied ways of overcoming most of these health-related problems.

The Reported Problems

The over 60 million people who use computers face many health problems that can be permanently physically and economically crippling.

Macworld reported in its January 1990 issue that almost a third of the readers who responded to a survey had experienced health problems they believed were related to computer use. Of these, 64 percent reported back or neck pain, 56 percent had eye problems, and another 12 percent had developed the strain injuries that come from repetitive motion. Most disturbing, 80 percent of *Macworld* subscribers using computers at work said their employers had failed to warn them of possible dangers.

Some ten states now regulate computer work, and most others are considering legislation. Many corporations are experiencing the consequences of employee awareness of the problems. At the Hertz Corporation in Oklahoma 20 percent of its data processors reported tendinitis because of the repetitive keyboarding of car rental contracts. Nearly half of the directory assistance operators at U.S. West Communications in Denver (the former Bell company) filed repetitive stress injury (RSI) claims.

Newspaper reporters across North America are suffering from RSI; at the *Los Angeles Times* alone, over 200 of the 1,100 members of the editorial staff sought medical help. Airline clerks, writers, office workers of all kinds, programmers, and many others who use computers are the first victims of what threatens to develop into an epidemic of computer-related medical problems, whether real or imaginary.

The National Institute for Occupational Safety and Health reports a rapidly increasing incidence of computer-related RSI problems, and that now more than half of all U.S. workers are exposed to RSI risk. Particularly vulnerable are over 20 million office workers who use a computer keyboard every day. The cost to corporations can range up to $100,000 or more per case in legal and medical expenses, lost time, and other cost consequences.

In addition, evidence is mounting of the potential hazards posed by radiation and electromagnetic fields created by video display terminals, particularly for pregnant women. Pending class-action suits on this issue alone make it an important management issue and may stimulate the use of LCD screens.

Not all computer-related health problems are of a physical nature. We have also the still largely unexplored consequences on our mental health and emotional states caused by difficult-to-use, frustrating software. Those stressors can set up damaging endorphin and other electrical and chemical interactions in our brains and central nervous systems. The situation is aggravated by software malfunctions, with program bugs that can be as stressful as a virus infection if they destroy or seriously interfere with our work. We need to be in good mental and physical health to withstand any stress, and a bad computing situation is a stressor itself.

Employees are not the only ones to suffer. Employers are being exposed to enormously expensive medical costs, liability claims, and disruption to their operations. Computer-related health problems collectively are draining U.S. businesses of billions of dollars a year. The liability exposure for employees will get increasingly expensive, as awareness of computer-related injuries spreads because of growing media attention. After all, this is the first industrial injury directly affecting opinion formers in the media, who virtually all use electronic editing systems.

The way that computing impacts on our health is a risk we can do much to control. When management tackles this problem in a constructive, coordinated way, benefits range from lower medical costs and reduced exposure to legal liability to considerably enhanced productivity and greater work quality.

There are less obvious psychological reasons why reducing stress among computer operators is highly cost-effective. The impact that your mental and physical state has on your relationship with any computer can exert a considerable influence over how successfully you ensure that the machine functions, and consequently how vulnerable it—and the work it does—is to all kinds of problems, from the many forms of operator error to the kind of carelessness that can increase the risk of virus infection.

If employees have a comfortable, pleasant working environment, with physical and mental stress minimized as much as possible, they are far more likely to have a positive relationship with their computer system and a better attitude about working. In many cases, it is easier to achieve this preferred situation with a portable computer than a desktop system.

There have been numerous cases of people trashing their desktop computers in anger when things go wrong. Computers have been kicked, thrown out of windows, hit with heavy objects, doused with water, shot, set on fire, and in other ways physically attacked.

In contrast, a phenomenon of the laptop computer is the way that users almost invariably regard their machines warmly as very personal possessions, often to the point of bonding, in which demonstrable symptoms of affection are displayed. Laptops have been elevated to join that exclusive category of inanimate objects that includes sports cars, jewelry, cameras, collectibles, and favorite clothing. The bond can be particularly strong for the road warrior, for whom a laptop is a constant companion through the stresses of business travel.

The use of laptops must be influenced by this unique relationship developing between men and women and these machines. The people most likely to be most productive at the keyboard are those who have warm feelings about the equipment they are using.

The attraction of laptops can only be enhanced as attention is focused on the most obvious negative aspects of computing: the health hazards, for which portable computers offer several solutions.

Change Your Work Environment and Your Work Habits

Computer users—both those of us who earn our living with the aid of computers and the over 30 million for whom they are a major leisure activity—are only now becoming aware of the serious health problems associated with computers. My computing, without my realizing it, deformed my body by reducing my neck movement by over 40 percent, causing severe head and neck pain, and doubling the rate at which my eyesight was deteriorating from natural aging. I am getting better, but it is a slow, painful, and expensive business.

My laptop plays an important role in my recovery. I use it to move around and change both my working position and my working environment, thereby eliminating much of the physical and mental stress caused by doing repetitive keyboarding in the fixed, undesirable position that most of us take unconsciously during long periods of concentration. By picking my computer up and taking my work to another place, I can get away from many stressors and blend work and pleasure into a higher-quality life-style. The laptop enables me to have far more control over my work environment.

The laptop is inherently less likely, because of its mobility and other features, to be blamed for the host of medical conditions that can be attributed to badly designed desks and even customized computer workstations.

Someone sitting with incorrect posture, in an unsatisfactory chair, with the desktop keyboard and monitor not in the ergonomically best positions can literally become crippled.

Symptoms develop slowly until, without warning, serious physical damage has resulted. Muscles go into spasms; nerves are pinched; excessive internal friction from hitting the keys up to 20,000 times an hour can literally seize up tendons in the wrists and arms.

Intense concentration without regular changes of position can lead directly to head, neck, and back problems—all with painful consequences. The positioning, adjustment, and type of monitor can cause head pain and eye disorders.

Of course, the laptop is not immune to causing some physical problems. But it has very low emission levels and does allow the user to adjust, consciously or unconsciously, his or her working environment. Often the portable computer really proves its worth by enabling the user to make a complete change of environment.

Enormous benefits can be obtained just by periodically working standing up. A University of California research project indicated mental productivity performance improvements of up to 30 percent when subjects worked standing. It is easy to lift the laptop to a higher working surface, something virtually impossible to do with a conventional desktop system, although you can achieve a lot by putting your monitor on a movable arm with a tilt-and-swivel platform and adding an extension cord to your keyboard.

Fortunately, the causes of most physical pain at the keyboard can be either eliminated or drastically reduced at little cost because of the portable's inherent flexibility.

An Ergonomic Workstation

One of the most effective ways of countering some of the health problems is to have an ergonomically correct workstation. This is nowhere near as difficult to achieve with a laptop as with a desktop computer.

It cost me $1,000 to get a workstation that gives just a few essential inches of up and down mobility to my desktop to ease my back and neck problems. Now I can improve—and vary—my working position and relationship to the monitor screen and keyboard. These system components are on an electric lift adapted from the mechanism for a sewing machine cabinet. I can raise or lower the keyboard and monitor, even to the extent of alternating between being seated and standing.

My unit, with the movable center section going up and down between two towers that contain my other computing needs, is ideal also for the handicapped confined to wheelchairs or beds. You roll the unit over a bed, like the rolling tables used in hospitals, or move a wheelchair beneath the center section, and adjust the keyboard and monitor to the most comfortable height.

Such a setup has particular relevance to laptop users because it can act as a very practical docking station as well. It will accommodate a monitor, printer, modem, and storage for disks and reference books, enabling even the low-cost laptops to double as effective desktop workstations. The workstation also enables the desktop and laptop to be used together, at the same time, for multitasking.

Such a workstation can be built by anyone reasonably competent with basic hand tools and customized easily to accommodate different equipment needs. More information is available from the International Computer Virus Institute, 1257 Siskiyou Boulevard, Suite 179, Ashland, Oregon 97520.

Other Solutions

People have tried other approaches to reducing pain at the keyboard. My Californian neighbor, sculptor Nick Cook, had really serious back problems from extensive computer work. He created a reclining workstation in a rocking chair that is suitable for either desktop or laptop systems. It is compact and portable—he uses it on his boat—and it has enabled him to work for up to eight hours at a time without pain. Nick has also created a range of innovative keyboard designs that are more comfortable for some people to use than the conventional keyboard.

I use a copy stand on an adjustable arm and a paper holder that fastens with Velcro strips to the side of my monitor. These devices enable me to position paper documents close to the monitor screen and in the same plane and at the same angle of view. This makes working much easier, but you need to remember to relax and exercise your eyes periodically by looking away from the screen at distant objects at the end of the room or out of the window.

Incidentally, on the subject of copy holders, if yours is made of metal and has magnetic devices to hold the paper in place, either be very careful or throw the magnets away. If anything magnetic—paperclip holders are another example—comes close to a disk, it can scramble the data. (That can happen even if you rest a disk against a telephone in a hotel room. When the phone rings, a magnetic field is created that can wreak havoc on the disk.)

Being able to change my work position frequently and getting timely medical treatment have saved me from serious, possibly permanent disability. After thirty years working as a writer, I was becoming deformed from bad posture at the keyboard. Fortunately, I consulted experts who helped me stand straight and get full mobility of my neck and head for the first time in a decade.

Problems for Laptop Users

Injuries you can be *more* prone to if you use a portable computer are those experienced by frequent business fliers carrying heavy laptops. There is a rapidly increasing incidence of back, neck, shoulder, and arm problems that can be traced to lugging a laptop on trips.

"Traveler's Elbow" involves pain which can travel from the elbow right up into the shoulder and neck, even causing headaches. It is caused by carrying briefcases, bags, or suitcases with our arms slightly bent. That strains the elbow joint, especially if the traveler is stressed and has tensed muscles.

So carry your portable with the arm extended and straight, allowing the much stronger shoulder muscles, not the elbow to take the load.

Laptop users walk long distances in airports with a heavy case slung over one shoulder. This puts your body out of balance and, if you are stiff and stressed, can actually cause muscle and joint injury that may not become apparent until later. As we saw in Chapter 10, putting your luggage—including your portable computer—on wheels is a practical way of reducing both the physical and mental stress of business travel.

Here are some additional tips to help avoid problems when using a portable computer.

- Reminders to exercise regularly can be built into many software programs. My word processor, like many these days, has a variable automatic SAVE feature. When that activates, I do a quick, now instinctive, check for stressors, vary my working positions, and exercise on every other SAVE.

- Your chair should have good lumbar and thigh support, and the seating position may be improved by having a small footstool, box, or a couple of thick telephone directories beneath your feet. This takes the weight off your thighs and helps blood circulate through your legs and feet. It is a useful tip for long flights, also. Do not, however, raise your feet so that your knees are elevated higher than your buttocks, which can cause other problems.

- Your chair should be adjustable even if the desk height is not, so that the keyboard can be reached easily from a relaxed position. Particularly avoid a high upwards reach, having to support the weight of your lower arms, wrists, and hands while pounding the keys.

- If you use a mouse, bring that within easy reach, also. I have an extension mouse platform on my slide-out keyboard shelf, and it has made a world of difference in increasing my productivity and in reducing stress.

- A wrist rest can be beneficial, but must not isolate hand from arm movements. They are now available commercially, or you can make one yourself for next to nothing. Experiment to see if it helps you. I made mine from a length of plastic foam pipe insulation costing under a dollar from my local hardware store. Cut it to length, slit it lengthwise, and slip it over the front edge of a keyboard drawer, table, or desk. My length of foam pipe doubles on trips as a convenient way of carrying spare batteries, which fit snugly along the space down the middle.

- Your screen should be positioned just a bit farther away than you would normally hold a newspaper or book, and angled so that you can look at it for long periods while maintaining good posture and without strain.

- Much eye strain stems from having unwanted glare or reflections in the screen. Position the computer so that it does not catch stressful light. Usually being at right angles to a window is better than either facing toward or away from it. It may take time to get used to the brightness and contrast of backlighting and the positioning of the main ambient light sources to make your portable's screen easiest to read.

- Light, particularly from strong ceiling fixtures, is necessary for efficient work with paper but generally is too bright for computing. So it may help to douse or lower the intensity of overhead lights if you can and use more controllable desktop lamps.

- Keep blinking regularly when computing, especially if you wear contact lenses. We tend to get so engrossed that we stare at the monitor without blinking as we would normally. The result is that the eye's natural lubrication system does not function. Your eyes become dry and irritated, increasing their vulnerability to strain and infection. So develop the habit of blinking every three or four seconds, and keeping your eyes closed fully at regular intervals until you feel them become moistened. (Contact lens wearers are particularly vulnerable to dry eye problems, but all computer users can benefit from the tips by Dr. Ernest Loewenstein in the free booklet available from the Polymer Technology Corporation, a contact lens manufacturer, 100 Research Drive, Wilmington, Massachusetts 01887. Called *VDT Users: Improve Comfort with the Blink of an Eye*, it contains a four-week regimen of exercises that form very effective calisthenics for the eyes and can help to prevent computer-related vision problems.)

Above all, keep moving regularly when computing for long periods, whether you are using a desktop, workstation, or portable. Take a short break two or three times every hour, and do some stretching exercises. These breaks and stretches used to happen automatically before computers, when we had to manually turn the carriage up to the next line or reach for a new piece of paper. But now we seem to work more efficiently with a minimum of physical movement, which may result in a short-term saving of time and effort but can create long-term health problems.

At the very least, stretch your fingers and do neck rolls to reduce the static muscle loading that results from extended periods of repetitive activity. The consequences of not doing so are by no means imaginary. If you sit for hours at the keyboard, barely moving your position, the circulation in your muscles is drastically reduced. This causes a buildup of waste products in your muscles that can lead to real pain. Nerves and tendons get pinched also, and the cumulative effect can be very serious.

Having an ergonomically efficient working position that you change often will enable you to do more work more comfortably. It will enhance your attitude toward using a computer and will keep you more motivated, less stressed, and happier. It will also help reduce the main reason that systems crash and data are lost: operator error.

Appendix C

Electronic Mail and Bulletin Boards

When you have got the communications hardware and software to make a connection, who should you call? A high proportion of experienced portable computer users find that electronic mail is their most valued communications facility. Indeed, for some it is the sole justification for taking a computer on a trip. Also invaluable can be the many on-line information services, while thousands of special-interest bulletin boards can be priceless sources of shareware programs, social and business contacts, and practical help on computer and other issues.

E-mail can be almost whatever you want it to be. You can use it as direct exchange of information with your base office, as a way of joining together a group of portable computer users (members of a sales force, for example), or as an efficient way of conducting any business electronically by correspondence. It can also be used for a variety of social purposes and to broadcast messages of almost any kind to a large audience.

How does electronic mail work? You create the document on your computer in the normal way and then send it by modem and telephone line to the equivalent of a postal sorting office. It stays there, put into the appropriate mail slots of the addressees, who call in regularly to check their E-mail, just as one would go to the local post office to empty a postal box.

There are services that will send your message on, delivering it for you either physically or electronically. It can be retransmitted as hard copy or electronic facsimile (fax), as a telex (the modern equivalent of a telegram), or in other forms.

Some companies specialize in E-mail services; others offer it as one of many on-line facilities. E-mail is, for example, available on the CompuServe, Source, GEnie, Delphi, Prodigy, and other leading on-line information services, together with databases and bulletin boards. Payment is per message, by time, by special corporate subscription rate, or other formula.

E-mail services are rather fragmented at the moment, with different methods of operating and very different interfaces, so it is difficult to switch from one service to another. But that is changing.

Many companies operate their own E-mail networks, either through a commercial service which they pay to provide the facility and its maintenance, or as their own stand-alone system. An increasing number of companies are setting up their own bulletin boards—as centralized information clearinghouses—to which members send or from which they collect messages, data, programming, and other kinds of computerized information at any time, day or night.

A basic PC with a hard disk and shareware software can get a corporate bulletin board up and running for under $2,000—or even less if an older, redundant computer is used. A bulletin board is the lowest cost and one of the most effective ways of creating a communications network for any size business. It is particularly appropriate when an organization has portable computer users scattered over a wide area. A board can supplement and extend a local area network, or even remove the need for one.

There are over thirty thousand bulletin boards in the United States, plus a growing range of electronic mail and on-line information services. It is impossible to list them all, but here is a selection of voice contact numbers:

AT&T Mail	800/624-5672
CompuServe	800/848-8199
Exec-PC	414/789-4200
GE Information Services	800/638-9636
MCI Mail	800/444-6245
NewsNet	800/345-1301
Nexis	800/541-6886
Prentice-Hall OnLine	800/333-0431
American Telecomputing Corp.	516/764-5326
The Well	415/332-4335
Western Union EasyLink	800/779-1111

Of particular value to portable computer users is the Laptops RoundTable, a special-interest group on the GEnie service. It has over 150,000 members, who exchange tips, programs, and information about all kinds of portable computing topics. There is a bulletin board message system and over 2,000 program and information files you can download. Leading, well-managed on-line services like this have procedures to reduce the risk of virus infections.

Here is the dial-up procedure:

1. Hook up your computer and modem, and dial:

    1-800-638-8369

2. When the connection is made, type:

    HHH

3. The service will respond with:

    U# = .

4. You reply by typing in:

    XJM11855,TRAVSOFT

You will be asked a series of questions, including your credit card or checking account number for billing purposes. The LapTop Roundtable and most other GEnie services are covered by the basic on-line rate, which at the time of writing was $6 an hour in the United States at offpeak time and $18 for peak time (between 8 A.M. and 6 P.M. on weekdays). These are the rates for a 1200-baud connection; 2400-baud differs by going up to $10 an hour offpeak, while 300-baud connections drop to $5 an hour.

When your membership has been validated, you get to the Laptops RoundTable by the keyword:

LAPTOPS

or by the page number command:

MOVe 655.

This is just one of literally tens of thousands of places you can visit electronically with a portable computer and a modem. The modem is your passport to a whole world of on-line services, databases, bulletin boards, and special-interest groups.

Appendix D

Portable Computing and the Handicapped

Portable computing offers more opportunities to empower millions of handicapped people to extend and enhance the quality of their lives.

The federal government has imposed far-reaching requirements that handicapped persons not be discriminated against and allowed a reasonable opportunity to work. There are specific provisions to give the handicapped equal access to computing facilities. Also, the growing shortage of skilled or readily trained labor means that in the 1990s the business community must actively seek suitable people. The handicapped, along with the elderly, represent an enormous underutilized human resource in our society that will help fill our labor needs.

In an increasing number of situations, the potential recruits with disabilities that seemingly cannot be overcome to the degree necessary to equip them for a particular vacancy will pull out their own portable system at the interview to demonstrate conclusively that they can fit the job function.

At the heart of these socially and economically important developments are the obvious benefits that are a direct consequence of computers having acquired mobility, plus the enormous progress being made in blending portable hardware with adaptive software. Now we have a new form of work-to-go—adaptive systems to go.

An adaptive computer system is one that has the ability to learn, enabling it to react to a variety of stimuli to carry out instructions or to change itself to meet different circumstances, such as a change in its environment or in the system's own state.

This extends the applications for the talking portable computer, opening dramatically wider horizons for the blind, the deaf, and those with other sight, speaking, and hearing impairments. Most laptops—all the battery-powered Toshibas, for example—can be equipped to talk to blind users.

The hardware element of a speech-synthesizer package can be contained on a card that fits into an internal expansion slot. The modem card slot is the favored location with the Toshibas and many units are designed specifically for this. Also, there are external hardware packages that can be hooked up to portables with sufficient memory by using either the communications or the printer port. The best of these, with unlimited vocabulary, are not much bigger than a cigarette pack and they connect to virtually any serial port.

The accompanying software is primarily a memory-resident package that intercepts the signals being sent either to the screen or originating from the keyboard, and redirects them to the voice synthesizer. These packages are now so good that they can adapt themselves very quickly to different operators and to different commercial or specially written applications programs.

For example, a blind person using Lotus 1-2-3 can get a voice message from the computer saying which cell is being worked in and verbalize back the data that is being inputted. Standard word processing software is controlled in a similar way, enabling an experienced user to enter text and manipulate it with menus to very high levels of proficiency.

Many blind users are so proficient at a keyboard in applications such as writing text that they input very rapidly without the need for much audible assistance. The voice-synthesizer facility is used mainly for checking and retrieving the data that have been computerized.

The cost of making a computer talk can be well under $1,000 for quite a sophisticated system, and the field is very competitive so prices are falling as the technology gets better.

The blind have a range of other options, including a portable Braille display that fits underneath the laptop and portable printers to yield Braille hard copy.

There are increasingly powerful devices that are getting smaller and more portable all the time, with the capacity to turn ordinary printed material into computerized data that can be used by the handicapped. Portable character-recognition scanners can read a book or other document into an ordinary PC with a hard drive and the computer will read it aloud.

Blind singer Stevie Wonder always travels with his talking book equipment.

As portables get smaller and more proficient, they are empowering the handicapped to be far more equal players in the information age. The blind can, for example, make telephone calls more easily. They can take their electronic sense expanders and substitutes from courtrooms to board meetings to college lecture halls for easy, on-the-spot note taking and access to references. In fact, handicapped students are on the cutting edge of technology making portable computers help in the learning process.

The partially sighted can get similar benefits even more easily and at lower cost with memory-resident software that enlarges the text on the screen by as much as 24 times—something many of us will find useful, especially as we get older. These large-print programs are a great way of turing a laptop into a teleprompter to make a speaker's notes easy to refer to, even in a darkened room during a screen presentation.

Of course, voice recognition and synthesizing have many other applications not restricted to the handicapped, especially in the kind of work situations where it is difficult or impossible to input or receive output in the conventional way via keyboard and screen.

There are adaptive systems that can learn new voice commands in just a few minutes, and will store this customized vocabulary in a form that enables even sophisticated graphics programs to be controlled entirely by vocal commands. So a quadriplegic with no limb movement can run CAD programs, make telephone calls, access databases, and use other information resources to be a fully functional engineer, designer, or executive. Or an engineer or researcher, whether handicapped or not, can record and receive data in almost any situation without needing to touch or see his computer. Those later applications can range from deep mining thousands of feet under the ground to controlling jet aircraft up in the air.

The possibilities of using portable computers to enhance the quality of life and the work capacity of the handicapped are increasing all the time. Because much machinery in our homes and workplaces is computer controlled, the portables that substitute for lost human abilities can extend their usefulness by directly interfacing with machines that do physical tasks. The blind and the physically impaired can now, with the help of their portables, control many industrial processes and perform most office functions. For example, using adaptive technology, portables can control robotic devices and wheelchairs.

Standard portables with no modifications or special peripherals can be used with software that helps dyslexics learn to read. The computer recognizes the reading-disabled person's voice and then human and machine can interact as they go through special learning programs that use graphic devices, including animation and speech, to teach understanding of the letter clusters that build into words.

Some of the "assistive technology" that aids the handicapped seems expensive. For example, PRAB Command and Zenith Data Systems have developed a workstation for quadriplegics that, with its advanced robotic devices, can cost around $50,000. But that can be cheap compared to the savings in the lifetime cost when a severely handicapped person is transformed from a community liability into an asset.

It is not necessary to spend large amounts to achieve substantial benefits. There are comprehensive voice-recognition systems costing under $200, suitable for portables that take standard cards.

Among the resources for further information are:

American Foundation for the Blind	212/620-2041
Heath/Zenith	616/383-4400
Enabling Technologies	305/283-4817
Digital Equipment	617/654-1500
Talking Computer Systems	617/926-1919
Visionware Software	617/437-3704

If you are involved with a nonprofit organization that needs help to use computers effectively, or have computing expertise you are prepared to share, the CompuMentor Project could be just what you are seeking. Based in San Francisco, it is now generating international interest as a way of achieving, in the words of its own slogan, "People Helping Computers Help People." The organization brings computer expertise together with the nonprofit organizations that can put it to good use. You do not have to be a computer specialist to be a volunteer mentor; just being computer literate can be enough. Details are available from the program director, Randy Dunagan, at (415) 255-6040.

Appendix E

Dedicated Word Processors vs. Portable Computers

The most popular portable computing activity is processing words. The most economical tool for doing that is the dedicated word processing machine. These machines tend not to be taken seriously by computer experts. But, in fact, they can be an excellent choice for certain applications.

Many journalists were pioneers in portable word processing, with Radio Shack's primitive (by present standards) word processing notebooks that they could carry anywhere. With a modem and acoustic coupler, they could zap copy back to their office from the nearest telephone.

The current generation of journalists is moving on to fully featured portables that aid their research in many ways. Led by pioneers such as Professor Jim Brown, Director of Indiana University's School of Journalism Institute for Advanced Reporting, more journalists are using portable computers to collect and process data while out in the field, not just to write their stories.

This is a classic example of how experience with portability expands the range of computer usage—and why it can be most disadvantageous to go with a dedicated system to meet an immediate need and not consider potential future requirements as your computing horizons expand. However, the other side of the coin is that some journalists have retained the same low-power portable word processor for years because it is familiar equipment that does a useful job; the returns that would come from upgrading do not justify the expense or time required to learn a new system.

There are dedicated word processors with the ability to do simple spreadsheets, create databases, and handle communications; most now also have mail merge and spell-check features. But a dedicated system has limited ability to grow in usefulness. It traps you in time because you cannot use the rapidly developing software that makes a general purpose computer able to process words with increasing proficiency as programs are upgraded.

Dedicated word processors also trap you in functions: you cannot, with a few limited exceptions, get your dedicated machine to do other tasks. It is rather like buying a hammer to undertake a job around the house, and then finding halfway through that you also need a screwdriver. The dedicated word processor will always be a hammer, of little use for anything other than driving in nails, while the general purpose computer of even modest specification can give a reasonable performance as a hammer, then switch easily to drive in screws if that is required later.

Consequently, there is no good in having a great word processor if your portable work requires you to create spreadsheets. But if you need only to crunch words and want the most power to do this for the fewest bucks, there are some great deals in this sector.

The lower cost of a dedicated word processor is attractive if your work pattern lends itself to having a number of systems at different locations, rather than taking portable equipment around with you. For example, a part-time secretary who goes to the office of three clients to process their correspondence could have a dedicated word processor in each place, with the capacity to print good-quality business letters, for less cost than a single laptop and printer he or she might carry along at considerable inconvenience.

Typewriter Substitutes

The dedicated word processor market starts with a wide choice of portable electronic typewriters that may claim to be word processors but have very limited capacity. Street prices can start at around $100 and go up to several hundred dollars, as features increase.

Memory is usually very limited—perhaps only a line or a page at a time—and the screen displays are tiny. Some electronic typewriters do have facilities for expanding memory and checking spelling, and the printout from those that use daisywheels can be of high quality, if slow. Most use either rechargeable or disposable standard batteries that cost little and are available everywhere, so this enhances their appeal for some people.

Do not consider this category unless you are certain you can live with the severe limitations of intermediate technology that brings only the basic features of word processing to typewriters. The next step up need not cost much, if any, more, and the additional benefits are enormous.

CRT Displays and Integral Printers

True word processors vary widely in specification and size. The cheapest can deliver high performance at very low initial cost if you do not need full portability. These are the square, box-shaped machines that use conventional cathode ray tube (CRT) display screens, have daisywheel printers built in, and include large keyboards that are usually detachable. Examples are the Panasonic 1500 range, the Magnavox Videowriter, and the Brother WP-80.

They are heavy—some over twenty pounds—and bulky, even those fitted with handles are as awkward to move around as the early transportable computers were. Some don't pretend to be truly mobile, but they still put all the basic word processing and printing requirements into a package that is compact enough to be moved from place to place far more easily than a desktop with its peripherals.

They rely on electricity because of their power-hungry CRT displays, but you can run them off external batteries through adapters and inverters— for example, from a car cigarette lighter socket.

These large word processors can pack in a lot of features. Their screens and keyboards generally are much better for intensive typing than on the typical laptop, and their prices have dropped to make them remarkable values if they suit your needs.

They have not been a great commercial success, partly because the market has not been well informed about their advantages and limitations. So these integrated word processors and printers are being deeply discounted, some discontinued, so you need to be sure that supplies and service will remain available.

For under $400 from the mail order discounters you can get a word processor with an excellent black on white—or white on black—nine-inch CRT screen, spell checker, unlimited external document storage on floppy disks, first-rate daisywheel printing, and such basic word processing features as auto pagination, search and replace, ability to move blocks of text, and mail merge. Some of them will also do spreadsheets; a few do other computerized tasks.

These word processors can be a practical, low-cost choice for a home office, as a way to increase secretarial productivity, for freelance writers whose publishers do not demand copy on disk, and for personal correspondence. However, they do not exchange data readily—or at all—with other systems, and are not easily portable—certainly not to be carried any distance or onto aircraft.

LCD Screens and Integral Printers

More versatile and portable word processing options are the smaller machines with LCD (liquid crystal display) screens and integrated daisywheel printers. They look like more sophisticated versions of the portable electronic typewriters described earlier, but the better ones have far superior displays showing several lines of text, larger and more substantial keyboards, and electronics with greater processing and memory capabilities.

Street prices for these range from about $500 to $900, and manufacturers include Smith-Corona, Panasonic, and Brother. They are far more portable than those using CRT displays, being more compact and weighing from about ten pounds to just under twenty pounds. They use a variety of ways of storing text, although even when done on a 3.5-inch microfloppy, don't expect to be able to run it in your laptop or desktop computer system. The floppies may fit the drive door, but they talk a very different computing language for which no translation is readily available. If you want to convert the text to proper computer processing, you will need—with a few exceptions—to print out a hard copy and scan it into the computer with optical character recognition equipment.

If they are to survive and prosper, this category of word processors must gain the ability to exchange data with computers. A pioneering step in this direction was the Smith-Corona PWP 7000 model range, which uses its own unique disk system but can convert its files into ASCII text for sending by modem or transferring by direct communications to a laptop or PC.

A useful portability feature is that the printer is a separate unit from the processor, screen, and keyboard, enabling the system to be trimmed from seventeen pounds to one nonprinting word processor module weighing under seven pounds that looks and feels much like a small laptop. It will also run a modest spreadsheet and can be fitted with a rechargeable power pack.

With both truly portable word processing and printing in a flexible two-part package for under $1,000, this type of word processor can meet many work-to-go needs at an attractive price.

Notebook Size Without Integral Printers

Even smaller and more portable are the dedicated word processors without printers, weighing under three pounds and able to fit in a large pocket or small briefcase. They are really not-so-smart notebook computers able to do only word processing and associated tasks.

Typical is the Tandy WP series, with an 80-column-by-8-row LCD screen. Its 62-key keyboard, built-in word processor, spell checker, thesaurus, and communications software are contained in a package the size of a sheet of letter paper and only an inch thick. It sells for around $350, often less on special offers.

These word processors are able to output to a variety of printers and communications devices through standard serial and parallel ports, so they can form flexible, portable stand-alones or extensions to a desktop or larger laptop system.

They do not have their own printers, unlike larger machines, and so are not fully integrated word processing systems, but their smaller size, long battery life, and portability are appealing. While they may look almost identical to portable computers of the same size, they restrict your opportunities for work-to-go to the processing of words.

Appendix F

Resources for Portable Computing

The portable computing industry is a highly competitive, fast-moving sector. New products are introduced daily; price structures fluctuate more than in most industries because of the frequent product changes. Often inventory becomes available at very attractive prices direct from manufacturers because a new version is being introduced.

Software publishers are particularly keen to get their programs introduced to a corporate environment, so they may make special efforts to help with training, in customizing features, or simply being more competitive in their pricing.

Special needs may be best met by small, specialist suppliers, but these can be difficult to locate. Often suppliers will work with customers to develop and test specialist applications, and such collaboration can be very cost-effective.

For these and many other reasons, acquiring a portable computing system can be a demanding, time-consuming task, needing quality information and good contacts for resources. To make that task easier, here is a comprehensive list of suppliers of portable computers, peripherals, supplies, and software, reproduced by permission of Portable Technology *update*. Subscribers receive such a list, revised and updated, every quarter; call (718)318-3880 for details.

3X USA One Executive Dr Fort Lee, NJ 07024	800-327-9712 201-592-6874	Communications
Above Software 3 Hutton Centre Suite 950 Santa Ana, CA 92707	714-545-1181	Software
Adtron 745 N Gilbert Rd #124 BX361 Gilbert, AZ 85234	602-940-0060	Access/Supplies/ Upgrades
Advanced Electronic Supp Prod 1801 NE 144th St N Miami, FL 33181	800-446-2377 305-944-7710	Access/Supplies/ Upgrades
Agilis Corp 1101 San Antonio Rd Mountain View, CA 94043	415-962-9400	Computers
Alpha Software Corp One North Ave Burlington, MA 01803	617-229-2924	Software
Alps Electric Company Inc 3553 N First St San Jose, CA 95134	408-432-6000	Peripherals (OEM Sales Only)
Altima Systems Inc 1390 Willow Pass Rd St 1050 Concord, CA 94520	800-356-9990 415-356-5600	Computers
Aluminum Case Company 3333 W 48th Place Chicago, IL 60632	313-247-4611	Access/Supplies/ Upgrades
American Cryptronics Inc 1580 Corporate Dr - St 123 Costa Mesa, CA 92626	714-540-1174	Access/Supplies/ Upgrades
Amherst International Corp 540 N Commercial St Manchester, NH 03101	800-547-5600 603-644-3555	Access/Supplies/ Upgrades

Reprinted with permission by Portable Technology *update*, 125 Beach 124th St., Belle Harbor, N.Y. 11694. (718) 318-3880.

Amica 1800 Busse Highway Des Plaines, IL 60016-6727	800-888-8455 312-635-5700	Software
Amstrad Inc 1915 Westbridge Dr Irving, TX 75038	214-518-0668	Computers
Apollo Audio Visual 60 Trade Zone Dr Ronkonkoma, NY 11779	800-777-3750 516-467-8033	Peripherals
Apple Computer Inc 2025 Mariani Ave Cupertino, CA 95014	408-996-1010	Computers
Applied Creative Technology 8333 Douglas Ave - Suite 700 Dallas, TX 75225	800-433-5373 214-739-4200	Software/ Peripherals
Areal Technology 580 College Ave Palo Alto, CA 94306	408-954-0360	Peripherals (OEM Sales Only)
Aristotle Industries Inc 3226 Beta Av Burnaby - BC, Canada V5G 4K4	800-663-2237 604-294-1113	Peripherals
Astro Systems 807 Aldo Ave #106 Santa Clara, CA 95054	408-727-7626	Peripherals
Asyst 29-33 West 36th St New York, NY 10018	212-239-0212	Services
Atari Corporation 1196 Borregas Ave Sunnyvale, CA 94088	408-745-2000	Computers
Avatar Corp 65 South St Hopkinton, MA 01748	800-289-2526 508-435-3000	Peripherals

Axonix Corp 2257 S 1100 E - Suite 2C Salt Lake City, UT 84106	800-866-9797 801-466-9797	Peripherals/ Access/Supplies/ Upgrades
Bay Technical Associates Inc 200 N Second St Bay St St. Louis, MO 39520	800-523-2702 601-467-8231	Peripherals
Bea Maurer Inc 14522-E Lee Rd Chantilly, VA 22021	703-631-6363	Access/Supplies/ Upgrades
Bi-Link Computer Inc 11606 East Washington Blvd Whittier Park, CA 90606	213-692-5345	Computers
Bi-Tech Enterprises Inc 10 Carlough Rd Bohemia, NY 11716	516-567-8155	Computers
Bluelynx 63 Maple St PO Box 335 Friendsville, MD 21531	301-746-5888	Communications
Bondwell Industrial Co 47485 Seabridge Dr Fremont, CA 94538	415-490-4300	Computers
Borland 1800 Green Hills Rd Scotts Valley, CA 95066	408-438-1869	Software
Broadax Systems Inc 4440 Telstar Ave Suite 4 El Monte, CA 91731	800-872-4547 818-442-0020	Computers
Buhl Industries Inc 14-01 Maple Ave Fairlawn, NJ 07410	201-423-2800	Peripherals
Bull AG 200 Smith St Waltham, MA 02154	617-895-6929	Computers
Business Works 5505 Morehouse Dr #150 San Diego, CA 92121	619-455-6094	Software

Reprinted with permission by Portable Technology *update*, 125 Beach 124th St., Belle Harbor, N.Y. 11694. (718) 318-3880.

Cables To Go 28 W Nottingham Dayton, OH 45420	800-826-7904 513-275-0886	Access/Supplies/ Upgrades
California Access 780 Montague Expressway #403 San Jose, CA 95131	408-435-1445	Peripherals
Cambridge North America 424 Cumberland Ave Portland, ME 04101	207-761-3700	Computers
Casio Inc 570 Mt. Pleasant Ave Dover, NJ 07801	201-361-5400	Computers
CenTech 1375 W St - 8040 South West Jordan, UT 84088	801-255-3999	Access/Supplies/ Upgrades
Chaplet Systems USA Inc 252 N Wolfe Rd Sunnyvale, CA 94086	408-732-7950	Computers
Cherry Corporation 3600 Sunset Ave Waukegan, IL 60087	312-662-9200	Access/Supplies/ Upgrades/Peripherals
Chicago Case Company 4446 South Ashland Ave Chicago, IL 60609	312-927-1600	Access/Supplies/ Upgrades
Chicony / Digicom Technology 307 W. Centrall St Natick, MA 01760	800-344-4211 508-820-1102	Computers
Chicony America Inc 1641 W Colins Ave Orange, CA 92667	714-771-6151	Computers
Chicony America Inc 1637 Stelton Rd Piscataway, NJ 08854	201-819-8300	Computers

Reprinted with permission by Portable Technology *update*, 125 Beach 124th St., Belle Harbor, N.Y. 11694. (718) 318-3880.

Chinon America Inc 660 Maple Ave Torrance, CA 90503	213-533-0274	Peripherals
Chips and Technologies, Inc 3050 Zanker Rd San Jose, CA 95134	408-434-0600	Access/Supplies/ Upgrades (OEM Sales Only)
Chisholm 910 Campisi Way Campbell, CA 95008	800-888-4210 408-559-1111	Peripherals
Chronologic Corp 5151 N Oracle Suite 210 Tucson, AZ 85704	602-293-3100	Software
Cirrus Logic Inc 1463 Centre Point Dr Milpitas, CA 95035	408-945-8305	Access/Supplies/ Upgrades (OEM Sales Only)
Club American Technologies 3401 West Warren Ave Fremont, CA 94539	415-490-2201	Computers
CMS Enhancements 1372 Valencia Ave Tustin, CA 92680	714-259-9555	Software/ Peripherals
Coherent Systems 42 Peck Slip New York, NY 10038-1713	212-285-1864	Software
Coker Electronics 1430 Lexington Ave San Mateo, CA 94402	415-573-5515	Communications
Colby Systems 2991 Alexis Dr Palo Alto, CA 94304	415-941-9090	Computers
COMCO SA Route de Lausanne 128 Le Mont, Switzerland 1052	021-365105	Communications

Reprinted with permission by Portable Technology *update*, 125 Beach 124th St., Belle Harbor, N.Y. 11694. (718) 318-3880.

Commax Technologies Inc 721 Charcot Ave San Jose, CA 95131	408-435-5000	Computers
Comnet 110 U.S. South North Brunswick, NJ 08902	201-821-6767	Peripherals
Compaq Computer Corporation 2055 FM 149 Houston, TX 77070	713-370-0670	Computers
Compuquest Inc 801 Morse Ave Schamburg, IL 60193	312-529-2552	Peripherals
Compuserve 5000 Arlington Century Blvd Columbus, OH 43220	800-848-8199 614-457-8600	Software/Services
Computer Accessories Corp 6610 Nancy Ridge Dr San Diego, CA 92121	800-582-2580 619-457-5500	Peripherals
Computers Products Plus 16321 Gothard St Unit F Huntington Beach, CA 92647	714-847-1799	Access/Supplies/ Upgrades
Connect Computer 9855 W 78th St. - Suite 270 Eden Prairie, MN 55344	612-944-0181	Peripherals
Conner Peripherals 3018 Zanker Rd San Jose, CA 95134-2128	408-433-3340	Peripherals (OEM Sales Only)
Contact Software International 9208 W Royal Lane Irving, TX 75063	800-627-3958 214-929-4749	Software
Crosstalk Communications 1000 Holcomb Woods Parkway Roswell, GA 30076	404-998-3998	Software

Reprinted with permission by Portable Technology *update*, 125 Beach 124th St., Belle Harbor, N.Y. 11694. (718) 318-3880.

CT & M Ltd 80 Burns Pl Suite A Goleta, CA 93117	804-683-1148	Access/Supplies/ Upgrades
CTXT Systems Inc 9205 Alabama Ave Chatsworth, CA 91311	818-341-4227	Computers
Custom Design Technology Inc 780 Montague Expressway San Jose, CA 95131	408-432-8698	Computers
CWW Inc 3 University Pl PO Box 185 Great Neck, NY 11022	212-267-1941	Access/Supplies/ Upgrades
D-Link Systems Inc 3303 Harbor Blvd - E8 Costa Mesa, CA 92626	714-549-7942	Communications
Data General Corp 4400 Computer Dr Westboro, MA 01580	800-DATA-GEN 508-366-8911	Computers
Datavue Corp One Meca Way Norcross, GA 30093	404-564-5555	Computers
Dauphin Technology 1125 E St Charles Rd Lombard, IL 60148	800-782-7922 312-627-4004	Computers
Dayflo Software 8013 Sky Park Circle E Irvine, CA 92714	800-367-5369 714-474-1364	Software
Dell Computer Corporation 9505 Arboretum Austin, TX 78759	800-426-5150 512-343-3450	Computers
Delta Computers Corp 300 N Continental Blvd #200 El Segundo, CA 90245	213-322-4222	Computers

Reprinted with permission by Portable Technology *update*, 125 Beach 124th St., Belle Harbor, N.Y. 11694. (718) 318-3880.

Delta Technology International 1621 Westgate Rd Eau Claire, WI 54703	800-242-6368 715-832-7575	Software
DFM Research & Development 1776 - 22nd St West Des Moines, IA 50265	515-225-6744	Computers
Diamond Flower Inc 7923 NW 21st St Miami, FL 33126	305-477-1988	Communications
Digital Products Inc 108 Water St Watertown, MA 02172	800-243-2333 617-924-1680	Communications/ Peripherals
Digital Systems 7959 178th Pl NE Redmond, WA 98052	206-881-7544	Access/Supplies/ Upgrades
Diversified Technology 112 East State St Ridgeland, MS 39158	800-443-2667 601-856-4121	Access/Supplies/ Upgrades
Dolch 2029 O'Toole Ave San Jose, CA 95131	800-538-7506 408-435-1881	Computers
Doradus Corp 6095 E River Rd Minneapolis, MN 55432	800-538-3008 612-572-1000	Computers/ Communications
Drive Phone Inc 37 Springvalley Ave Paramus, NJ 07652	201-843-6400	Access/Supplies/ Upgrades/ Communications
Dukane Corporation 2900 Dukane Dr St. Charles, IL 60174	800-634-2800 312-584-2300	Peripherals
Dynabrook Technologies 1751 Fox Dr San Jose, CA 95131	415-847-0660	Computers
Dynamac Computer Products 555 17th St Suite 1850 Denver, CO 80202	303-296-0606	Computers

Reprinted with permission by Portable Technology *update*, 125 Beach 124th St., Belle Harbor, N.Y. 11694. (718) 318-3880.

Dynatron Associates Inc 5880 W Las Positas Blvd #49 Pleasanton, CA 94566	415-734-0560	Computers
Eastman Kodak Company 343 State St Rochester, NY 14650	716-724-3169	Peripherals
Eastman Kodak Company 343 State St Rochester, NY 14650	716-724-3000	Peripherals
ECA C & C Products 38 Route 46 East Lodi, NJ 07644	800-442-6872 201-478-0302	Peripherals
Eiki International 27882 Camino Capistrano Laguna Niguel, CA 92677	714-592-2511	Peripherals
Electronic Specialists 171 South Main St PO Box 389 Natick, MA 01760	800-225-4876 508-655-1532	Access/Supplies/ Upgrades
Elmo Manufacturing 70 New Hyde Park Rd New Hyde Park, NY 11040	516-775-3200	Peripherals
Enable Software Inc Executive Park Ballston Lake, NY 12019	518-887-8600	Software
Epson America Inc 2780 Lomita Blvd Torrance, CA 90505	800-922-8911 213-539-9140	Computers
Equinox Systems Inc 14260 S.W. 119th Ave Miami, FL 33186	800-DATA-PBX 305-255-3500	Peripherals
Fair Tide Technologies Inc 18 Ray Ave Burlington, MA 01803	617-229-6409	Software

Reprinted with permission by Portable Technology *update,* 125 Beach 124th St., Belle Harbor, N.Y. 11694. (718) 318-3880.

Fifth Generation Systems Inc 1120 Industriplex Blvd Baton Rouge, LA 70809-4112	800-225-2775 504-291-7221	Software
First Phase Inc PO Box 4504 Greensboro, NC 27404	919-855-8858	Software
Floor Covering Systems 5313 Silver Strand Way Sacramento, CA 95841	916-344-5175	Software
Form Maker Software 57 South Shillinger Rd Mobile, AL 33608	800-888-8423 205-633-3676	Software
Fortek Inc 240 James St Bensenville, IL 60106	312-595-2540	Computers
Fortis Information Systems 6070 Rickenbacker Rd Commerca, CA 90040	213-727-1227	Computers
Future Communications Systems 170 Broadway Suite 201 New York, NY 10038	212-903-5626	Computers
Gates Energy Products Highway 441 North Hague, FL 32615	904-472-4750	Batteries (OEM Sales Only)
GCC Technologies 580 Winter St Waltham, MA 02154	617-890-0880	Peripherals
Gemini Incorporated 103 Mensing Way Cannon Falls, MN 55009	507-263-3957	Access/Supplies/ Upgrades
GEnie's Laptops RoundTable 2308 Chetwood Circle #103 Timonium, MD 21093-2415	301-252-5379	Services

GetC Software Inc Box 8110-182 - 264 H St Blaine, WA 98230-8110	800-663-8066	Software
Gibson Research Corp 22991 La Cadena Laguna Hills, CA 92653	714-830-2200	Software
Giltronix Inc 1430 O'Brien Drive Bldg D Menlo Park, CA 94025	800-521-1330	Peripherals
GRiD Systems Corp 47211 Lakeview Blvd Box 5003 Fremont, CA 94537	800-222-GRiD 415-656-4700	Computers
GTE Mobile Communications 502 Old Country Rd Hicksville, NY	516-938-4700	Communications
GVC/Chenel Corp 99 Demarest Rd Sparta, NJ 07871	800-243-6312 201-666-1443	Communications
Hayes Microcomputer Products 705 Westeck Dr Norcross, GA 30092	404-449-8791	Communications
Hewlett-Packard 19310 Pruneridge Ave Cupertino, CA 95014	800-752-0900	Computers
Hitachi Office Automation Sys 6 Pearl Ct Allendale, NJ 07401	201-825-800	Computers
Holmes Microsystems 2620 South 900 West Salt Lake City, UT 84119	800-443-3034 801-975-9929	Communications
Husky Computers Inc 1133 4th St Sarasota, FL 34236	813-365-5180	Computers

Reprinted with permission by Portable Technology *update*, 125 Beach 124th St., Belle Harbor, N.Y. 11694. (718) 318-3880.

Hyundai Electronics America 166 Baypointe Parkway San Jose, CA 95134	408-473-9200	Computers
IBM 1133 Westchester Ave White Plains, NY 10604	800-IBM-2468	Computers
In Focus Systems Inc 7649 SW Mohawk St Tualatin, OR 97206	800-327-7231 503-692-4968	Peripherals
Inforite Corp 1670 S. Amphlett Blvd #201 San Mateo, CA 94402	415-571-8766	Computers
Information Machines 20219 Chapter Dr Woodland Hills, CA 91364	818-884-5779	Communications
Informer Computer Terminals 12781 Pala Dr Garden Grove, CA 92641	714-891-1112	Peripherals
Innovative Manufacturing Corp 3704 NW 82nd St Miami, FL 33147	800-950-2286 305-836-1035	Access/Supplies/ Upgrades
Input Systems 15600 Palmetto Lake Dr Miami, FL 33157	305-252-1550	Access/Supplies/ Upgrades
Intec Research Co 550 Cypress Ave Sunnyvale, CA 94086	408-732-3076	Peripherals
Intel Corporation 2625 Walsh Ave Santa Clara, CA 95052	408-765-4280	Access/Supplies/ Upgrades
Intelligence Technology Corp 16526 Westgrove Dallas, TX 75248	214-250-4277	Computers

Reprinted with permission by Portable Technology *update,* 125 Beach 124th St., Belle Harbor, N.Y. 11694. (718) 318-3880.

International Systems Mktng 943-A Russell Ave Gaithersburg, MD 20879	301-670-1813	Computers
Interpreter Inc 11455 West 48th Ave Wheat Ridge, CO 80033	303-431-8991	Peripherals
Irwin Magnetic Systems 2101 Commonwealth Blvd Ann Arbor, MI 48705	800-421-1879 313-324-3333	Peripherals
ISIS International 7100 N Broadway Suite 6L Denver, CO 80221	303-650-1492	Access/Supplies/ Upgrades
Itron East 15616 Euclid Ave Spokane, WA 99215	509-924-9900	Computers
Itron Inc 4505 S Wasatch Blvd Salt Lake City, UT 84124	801-272-6000	Computers
JW Systems Ltd 445 Broadhollow Rd Melville, NY 11747	800-242-8003	Software
Kalmar Designs 3303 Merrick Rd Wantagh, NY 11793	516-221-8400	Access/Supplies/ Upgrades
KAO Info Systems 10300 SW Nimbus Ave Portland, OR 97223	503-620-1888	Access/Supplies/ Upgrades
Kaypro 533 Stevens Ave Solana Beach, CA 92075	619-259-4789	Computers
Kelly Micro Systems 39 Musick Irvine, CA 92618	800-350-3900 714-859-3900	Access/Supplies/ Upgrades
Key Systems Inc 512 Executive Pk Louisville, KY 40207	502-897-3332	Software

Key Tronic Corporation B 4424 Sullivan Rd Spokane, WA 99216	509-928-8000	Peripherals
Kiss Computer Corporation 2604 Washington Rd Kenosha, WI 53140-2375	800-GET-KISS 414-694-KISS	Displays (OEM Sales Only)
Kres Engineering PO Box 1268 La Canada, CA 91011	818-957-1268	Peripherals
Maxtron 1825-A Durfee Ave S. El Monte, CA 91733	818-350-5705	Computers
MCI International 2 International Dr Rye Brook, NY 10573	800-444-6245	Services
Mead-Hatcher Inc P.O. Box 861 Buffalo, NY 14240	716-877-1185	Access/Supplies/ Upgrades
Medbar Enterprises Inc 71-08 51st Ave Woodside, NY 11377	718-335-0404	Communications
Megahertz Corp 4505 South Wasatch Blvd Salt Lake City, UT 84124	800-LAPTOPS 801-272-6000	Communications
Megapower Electronics 12 Winthrop Pl Staten Island, NY 10314	718-273-9560	Peripherals
Melard Technologies Inc 5 Odell Plaza Yonkers, NY 10701	914-376-0100	Computers
Micro Direct 2010 Revere Beach Park Everett, MA 02149	800-872-4286 617-387-2200	Computers
Micro Express 2114 S. Grand Ave Santa Ana, CA 92705	714-662-1973	Computers

Reprinted with permission by Portable Technology *update*, 125 Beach 124th St., Belle Harbor, N.Y. 11694. (718) 318-3880.

Micro Logic Corporation P.O. Box 70 Hackensack, NJ 07602	201-342-6518	Software
Micro Palm Computers 13773-500 Icot Blvd Clearwater, FL 34620	813-530-0128	Computers
Micro Slate 9625 Ignace Street Suite D Brossard, Quebec J4Y 2P3	514-444-3680	Computers
Microcom 500 River Ridge Dr Norwood, MA 02062	617-551-1957	Communications
Microcom Software Division 55 Federal Road Danbury, CT 06810	800-847-3529 203-798-3800	Software
Microguard 124 West 24th St Suite 6D New York, NY 10011	212-989-3972	Software
Microlytics Inc 1 Tobey Village Office Pk Pittsford, NY 14534	800-828-6293 716-248-9150	Software
Micron Technology 2805 East Columbia Rd Boise, ID 83706	800-Micron-1 208-386-3900	Access/Supplies/ Upgrades
Micronet Computer Systems 13525½ Alondara Blvd Sante Fe Springs, CA 90670	213-921-0068	Peripherals
MicroTouch Systems Inc 10 State St Woburn, MA 01801	617-935-0080	Peripherals
Midern Computers Inc 18005 Cortney Court City of Industry, CA 91748	818-350-0654	Access/Supplies/ Upgrades
Migent Inc 865 Tahoe Blvd Incline Village, NV 89450	702-832-3700	Communications

Reprinted with permission by Portable Technology *update,* 125 Beach 124th St., Belle Harbor, N.Y. 11694. (718) 318-3880.

Mission Cyrus Corp 18303 Eighth Ave South Seattle, WA 98148	604-432-7727	Computers
Misuba Corp 650 West Terrace Dr San Dimas, CA 91773	800-648-7822 714-592-2866	Computers
Mitsubishi Electronics 991 Knox St Torrance, CA 90502	800-556-1234 213-217-5732	Computers/ Peripherals
Modatech Systems Inc 910-1090 W Georgia St Vancouver, BC, Canada V6E 3V7	604-662-7272	Software
Mosaic 1972 Massachusetts Ave Cambridge, MA 02140	617-862-7148	Software
Mountain Computer Inc 240 Hacienda Ave Campbell, CA 95008	800-458-0300 408-379-4300	Peripherals
National Micro Systems Inc 2833 Peterson Pl Norcross, GA 30071	404-446-0520	Computers
NEC Home Electronics 1255 Michael Dr Wood Dale, IL 60191	312-860-9500	Computers/ Peripherals
NEC Information Systems Inc 1414 Massachusetts Ave Boxborough, MA 01719	508-264-8000	Computers/ Peripherals
NetLine 2155 N 200 West - Suite 90 Provo, UT 84604	801-373-6000	Software/ Peripherals
NS International Inc 4 Hills Park La Smithtown, NY 11787	516-366-0700	Access/Supplies/ Upgrades

Reprinted with permission by Portable Technology *update*, 125 Beach 124th St., Belle Harbor, N.Y. 11694. (718) 318-3880.

NTC Computer Corp 10613 Rush St South El Monte, CA 91733	818-401-9260	Peripherals
nView Corporation 11835 Canon Blvd - Suite C101 Newport News, VA 23606	804-873-1354	Peripherals
O'Neill Communications 100 Thanet Circle Princeton, NJ 08540	609-924-1095	Communications
Oak Technology Inc 139 Kifer Ct Sunnyvale, CA 94086	408-737-0888	Access/Supplies/ Upgrades (OEM Sales Only)
Office Solutions 2802 Coho St Madison, WI 53713	415-335-2035	Software
Ogivar Technologies 7200 Trans Canada Highway Quebec, Canada H4T 1A3	800-361-3694 514-737-3340	Computers
P.A.C.E. 180 South 600 West Logan, UT 84321	800-359-6670 801-753-1067	Access/Supplies/ Upgrades
Pace Mark Technologies Inc 3932 North Kilpatrick Ave Chicago, IL 60641	312-202-9700	Peripherals
Packard Bell 9425 Canoga Ave Chatsworth, CA 91311	818-773-4400	Computers
Panasonic One Panasonic Way Seacaucus, NJ 07094	201-348-7183	Peripherals
Paravant Computer Systems 305 East Drive W Melbourne, FL 32904	407-727-3672	Computers

PC Etcetera 450 Seventh Ave New York, NY 10123	212-736-5870	Services
PC-SIG 1030 D East Duane Ave Sunnyvale, CA 94086	800-245-6717 800-222-2996	Software
Phoenix Technologies 846 University Ave Norwood, MA 02062	671-551-4000	Peripherals (OEM Sales Only)
Poqet Computer Corp 650 N. Mary Ave Sunnyvale, CA 94086	408-737-8100	Computers
Portfolio Systems Inc 156 Flushing Ave Brooklyn, NY 11205	800-SAY-DYNO 718-935-9501	Software
Practical Peripherals 31245 La Baya Dr Westlake Village, CA 91362	800-442-4774 818-706-0333	Peripherals/ Communications
PrairieTek Corporation 1830 Lefthand Circle Longmont, CO 80501	800-825-2511 303-772-4011	Hard Disk Drives (OEM Sales Only)
Prime Solutions 1940 Garnet Ave San Diego, CA 92109	619-274-5000	Software
Printworx 3322 S. Memorial Parkway Huntsville, AL 35801	800-777-9679 205-880-3626	Access/Supplies/ Upgrades
Procomm Technology Inc 200 McCormick Costa Mesa, CA 92626	714-549-9449	Peripherals
Product R&D Corp 1194 Pacific St - St 201 San Luis Obispo, CA 93401	800-234-5584 805-546-9713	Communications/ Access/Supplies/ Upgrades
Prometheus Products Inc 7225 SW Bonita Rd Tigard, OR 97223	503-624-0571	Communications

Reprinted with permission by Portable Technology *update*, 125 Beach 124th St., Belle Harbor, N.Y. 11694. (718) 318-3880.

Protec Microsystems Inc 557 Lepine St Dorval, Quebec H9P 2R2	514-682-6461	Peripherals
Pure Data 1740 S 1-35 Suite 240 Carrollton, TX 75006	212-242-2040	Communications
Quadram/Asher One Quad Way Norcross, GA 30093	404-923-6666	Communications
Quasitronics Inc 211 Vandale Dr Houston, PA 15342	800-245-4192 412-745-2663	Peripherals
Quay Computer Corp 216 Matheson Blvd East Mississauga, Ontario L4Z 1X1	416-890-1956	Communications
Radix Corporation 4855 Wiley Post Way Salt Lake City, UT 84116	800-367-9256 801-537-1717	Computers/ Peripherals
Random Coporation 581 Northland Blvd Cincinnati, OH 45420	513-825-0880	Peripherals
RCI Mfg 2418 Warrington Dr Grand Prairie, TX 75052	214-641-8795	Peripherals
Reflection Technology 240 Bear Hill Rd Waltham, MA 02154	617-890-5905	Peripherals (OEM Sales Only)
Reliable Communications Inc 20111 Stevens Creek Blvd Cupertino, CA 95014	800-222-0042 408-996-0230	Peripherals
Richmond Software Inc 6400 Roberts St Suite 420 Burnaby, BC, Canada V5G 4C9	604-299-2121	Software

Reprinted with permission by Portable Technology *update*, 125 Beach 124th St., Belle Harbor, N.Y. 11694. (718) 318-3880.

Rick's RamStar Inc P.O. Box 759 Sardis, GA 30456	800-327-2303 305-233-1991	Access/Supplies/ Upgrades
Ricoh Corp 155 Passaic Ave Fairfield, NJ 07006	800-225-1899 201-882-2000	Peripherals
Rite Software 4144 N Central Expressway #530 Dallas, TX 75204	214-823-2978	Software
Rose Electronics P.O. Box 742571 Houston, TX 77274-2571	713-933-7673	Communications Peripherals
Rupp Corporation P.O. Drawer J New York, NY 10021	212-517-7775	Software
S.L.S. Technology 245 Pegasus Ave Northvale, NJ 07647	201-784-0987	Peripherals
SaleMaker Software Box 531650 Grand Prairie, TX 75053	800-433-5355 214-264-2626	Software
Samsung Information Systems 3725 N First St San Jose, CA 95134	800-642-7605 408-434-5482	Computers
Sanyo Business Systems Corp 51 Joseph St Moonache, NJ 07074	800-524-0046 201-440-9300	Computers
Scenario Inc 260 Franklin St - 5th Floor Boston, MA 02110	617-625-1818	Computers
Scherrer Resources Inc (SRI) 8100 Cherokee St Philadelphia, PA 19118	800-950-0190 215-242-8751	Software

Reprinted with permission by Portable Technology *update*, 125 Beach 124th St., Belle Harbor, N.Y. 11694. (718) 318-3880.

Scully Inc 725 E. Washington Blvd Los Angeles, CA 90021	213-748-3226	Access/Supplies/ Upgrades
Sealevel P.O. Box 1808 Easley, SC 29641	803-855-1581	Peripherals
Semi-Tech Microelectronics 131 McNabb Markham, Canada L3R 5V7	416-475-2670	Computers
Sharp Electronics Sharp Plaza Mahwah, NJ 07430-2135	201-529-8965	Computers
Simple Net Systems Inc 545 W Lambert Rd - Suite A Brea, CA 92626	714-529-8850	Communications
Ski Soft Publishing Corp 1644 Massachusetts Ave Lexington, MA 02173	800-662-3622 617-863-1876	Software
Softklone 336 Office Plaza Dr Tallahassee, FL 32301	904-878-8564	Communications
Software Link 3577 Parkway La Norcross, GA 30092	404-448-5465	Communications
Software Publishing Corp 1901 Landings Drive Box 7210 Mountain View, CA 94039	415-335-2080	Software
Sopris Softworks P.O. Box 916 Glenwood Springs, CO 81602	800-334-6046 303-945-0366	Access/Supplies/ Upgrades
Source One Systems 9234 FM 1960 West Houston, TX 77070	713-469-7000	Access/Supplies/ Upgrades

Reprinted with permission by Portable Technology *update,* 125 Beach 124th St., Belle Harbor, N.Y. 11694. (718) 318-3880.

Spectrum Cellular 800 N Tower 2700 Stemmons Dallas, TX 75207	214-630-9825	Communications
Sportcase Inc 610 13th Ave South Hopkins, MN	612-933-4545	Access/Supplies/ Upgrades
Spread Information Sciences 85-36 Grand Ave Elmhurst, NY 11373	718-397-1300	Computers (OEM Sales Only)
SRW Computer Co 18385 Bandilier Circle Fountain Valley, CA 92708	714-963-5500	Access/Supplies/ Upgrades
Statpower Technologies Corp 7012 Lockheed Highway Burnaby, BC, Canada V5A 1W2	604-420-1585	Access/Supplies/ Upgrades
Stone Bridge Luggage Inc 232 Washington Pl Wayne, PA 19807	215-647-8534	Access/Supplies/ Upgrades
Strong Group 105 Maplewood Ave Gloucester, MA 01930	502-281-3300	Access/Supplies/ Upgrades
Sunhill Inc 1000 Andover Park East Seattle, WA 98188	800-544-1361 206-575-4131	Adapters/Batteries/ Communications
Systems Peripherals 9747 Business Park Ave San Diego, CA 92131	800-345-0824 619-693-8611	Peripherals
Tallgrass Technologies 11100 West 82nd St Overland Park, KS 66214	800-825-4727 913-492-6002	Peripherals
Tandy Corporation 1700 One Tandy Way Fort Worth, TX 76102	817-878-4969	Computers

Reprinted with permission by Portable Technology *update*, 125 Beach 124th St., Belle Harbor, N.Y. 11694. (718) 318-3880.

Targus 6190 Walley View Buena Park, CA 90620	714-523-5429	Access/Supplies/ Upgrades
Tatung Company of America 2850 El Presidio St Long Beach, CA 90810	800-827-2850 213-637-2105	Computers
TEC Technological Evolution 603 Begonia Corona del Mar, CA 92625	714-723-4426	Access/Supplies/ Upgrades
Teknosys 3923 Coconut Palm Dr #111 Tampa, Fl 33619	813-620-3494	Software
TekPort Computer Center 1156 E Ridgewood Ave Ridgewood, NJ 07450	201-670-0777	Computers/ Peripherals
Telex Communication Inc 9600 Aldrich Ave S Minneapolis, MN 55420	612-887-8531	Peripherals
Telxon Corp 3330 West Market St Akron, OH 44313	800-537-5488 216-867-3700	Computers/ Peripherals
Tesco International Inc 2907 State Rd & 590 - #10 Clearwater, FL 34619	813-796-0300	Peripherals
Texas Instruments P.O. Box 202230 Austin, TX 78720	800-527-3500 512-250-6679	Peripherals
Toshiba America 9740 Irvine Blvd Irvine, CA 92718	800-423-4589 714-583-3000	Computers
Touchbase Systems Inc 160 Laurel Ave Northport, NY 11768	516-261-0423	Communications
Touchstone Technology Inc 955 Buffalo Rd Rochester, NY 14624	800-828-6968 716-235-8358	Peripherals

Reprinted with permission by Portable Technology *update*, 125 Beach 124th St., Belle Harbor, N.Y. 11694. (718) 318-3880.

Trans PC Systems 11849 E Firestone Blvd Norwalk, CA 90650	213-868-6930	Computers
Traveling Software 18702 N Creek Parkway Bothell, WA 98011	800-343-8080 206-483-8080	Software/ Peripherals
TVMP Inc P.O. Box 771869 Houston, TX 77215	800-762-3361 713-266-9779	Access/Supplies/ Upgrades
U.S. Micro Engineering 2810 Wilderness Pl Boulder, CO 80301	303-939-8700	Computers
U.S. Robotics 8100 N McCormick Blvd Skokie, IL 60076	312-982-5150	Communications
UCM Inc 13918 Equitable Rd Cerritos, CA 90701	213-404-5611	Computers
Ultrasoft Innovations Inc P.O. Box 247 Champlain, NY 12919	514-487-9293	Access/Supplies/ Upgrades
Unlimited Systems 9225 Chesapeake Dr Suite J San Diego, CA 92123	619-277-3300	Access/Supplies/ Upgrades
Valitek Mountain Farms Mall Hadley, MA 01035	413-586-7408	Peripherals
Veridata 11901 Goldring Rd #A & B Arcadia, CA 91006	818-303-0613	Computers
Vertisoft Systems Inc 100 California St #1400 San Francisco, CA 94111	415-956-6303	Software

Reprinted with permission by Portable Technology *update*, 125 Beach 124th St., Belle Harbor, N.Y. 11694. (718) 318-3880.

Videx Inc 1105 NE Circle Blvd Corvallis, OR 97330	503-758-0521	Peripherals
Visualon 3044 Payne Ave Cleveland, Ohio 44114	216-566-0506	Peripherals
Vital Communications 828 U.S. 46 West Parsippany, NJ 07054	201-334-2214	Communications
Wallaby Systems Inc 2540 Frontier Ave #109 Boulder, CO 80301	303-444-4606	Computers
Weltec digital inc 3002 W Dow Ave #132 Tustin, CA 92680	800-333-5155 714-669-1955	Peripherals
West Coast Telcom PO Box 230456 Portland, OR 97223	503-620-1888	Access/Supplies/ Upgrades
Western Digital 2445 McCabe Way Irvine, CA 92714	800-847-6181 714-863-0121	Communications
Western Telematic 5 Sterling Irving, CA 92718	714-586-9950	Peripherals/ Access/Supplies/ Upgrades
Western Union Corp 1 Lake St Upper Saddle River, NJ 07458	800-527-5184 201-818-5000	Services
White Crane Systems 6400 Atlantic Blvd - Ste 180 Norcross, GA 30071	800-344-6783 404-446-0660	Software
WordPerfect Corporation 1555 N Technology Way Orem, UT 84057	801-225-5000	Software
Xec Products 13575 58th St N Suite 123 Clearwater, FL 34620	813-538-4190	Computers

Reprinted with permission by Portable Technology *update*, 125 Beach 124th St., Belle Harbor, N.Y. 11694. (718) 318-3880.

Xecom   408-945-6640   Communications
374 Turquois Dr
Milpitas, CA 95035

Xircom   818-884-8755   Communications
22231 Mulhulland Highway
#114
Woodland Hills, CA 91364

Yamaha Corp of America   714-522-9963   Computers
6600 Orangethorpe Ave
Buena Park, CA 90620

Yamaha Systems   408-433-5260   Access/Supplies/
Technology Div   Upgrades
3051 North First St   (OEM Sales Only)
San Jose, CA 95134

Zenith Data Systems   312-699-4839   Computers
1000 Milwaukee Ave
Glenview, IL 60025

Zirco   303-421-2013   Access/Supplies/
10900 W 44th Ave   Upgrades
Wheat Ridge, CO 80033

Publication	Frequency	Publisher
Lap Gazette	Monthly	Boston Computer Society One Centre Plaza Boston, MA 02108 Membership: (617) 367-8080
Laptop & Portable Computer Express	Monthly	Portable Computing Int'l Corp P.O. Box 428 Peterborough, NH 03458-0428
MicroLife	Monthly	Toshiba MicroLife 275 Centennial Way, Suite 104 Tustin, CA 92680 Subscriptions: no phone orders

Reprinted with permission by Portable Technology *update*, 125 Beach 124th St., Belle Harbor, N.Y. 11694. (718) 318-3880.

PC Laptop Magazine	Monthly	LFP Inc 9171 Wilshire Blvd Suite 300 Beverly Hills, CA 90210 Subscriptions: (818) 760-8983
Portable 100	Bi-Monthly	Portable Computing International 145 Grove St Peterborough, NH 03458 Subscriptions: (603) 924-9455
Portable Computing	Monthly	IDG/Peterborough 80 Elm St Peterborough, NH 03458 Subscriptions: (800) 441-4403
Portable Paper	Bi-Monthly	Personalized Software P.O. Box 869 Fairfield IA 52556 Subscriptions: (515) 472-6330
Portable Technology *update*	Monthly	Portable Technology *update* 125 Beach 124th St Belle Harbor, NY 11694 Subscriptions: (718) 318-3880
Sales Topics	Quarterly	Sales Technologies 3399 Peachtree Rd NE Atlanta, GA 30326 Subscriptions: (404) 841-4000
Ultralite Connection	Bi-Monthly	Personalized Software P.O. Box 869 Fairfield, IA 52556 Subscriptions: (515) 472-6330

Reprinted with permission by Portable Technology *update*, 125 Beach 124th St., Belle Harbor, N.Y. 11694. (718) 318-3880.

Index

(Note: names and address details of source companies for computer products and services are listed alphabetically in Appendix F)

A CONSCIENCE CAN BE A HANDICAP ...

Swearengen was busy hating damned near everybody he could call to mind. They were all out to get him. Their goal was to make his life miserable, and they were doing a damned good job of it.

Not much longer, he told himself. He had made the deal with the Parkhurst woman because he wanted to be rid of Hickok before the famous gunman had a chance to pin on a marshal's badge and try to clean up Deadwood. Swearengen didn't want Deadwood cleaned up. He made his money from folks being dirty, and he wanted to keep it that way.

Parkhurst wanted Hickok dead, too, although she seemed equally interested in getting rid of Preacher Smith. The preacher was a damned nuisance, all right. He was bad for business, just like Hickok. In his own way, he might even be worse than Wild Bill, because he preyed on people's guilty consciences.

Swearengen was glad he had been born without one of those pesky things. It would have made his life even more difficult than it had been.

Berkley titles by Mike Jameson

The Tales from Deadwood series

TALES FROM DEADWOOD
THE GAMBLERS
THE KILLERS